HELP! FOR PARENTS

HELP! FOR PARENTS

Dr. Anthony J. LaPray
with Bob Greer

First Edition

1 2 3 4 5 6 7 8 9

Printed in the United States of America

Library of Congress Cataloging-in-Publication Data

LaPray, Anthony J., 1935-
Help! for parents.

1. Parenting 2. Child psychology I. Greer, Bob, 1950- . II. Title.
HQ755.8.L363 1986 649'.1 86-17054
ISBN 0-87108-718-9 (pbk.)

Book and cover design by Signorella Graphic Arts

To our parents and our children—the links that keep the chain strong.

Help! For Parents

Contents

Foreword

Parenting doesn't have to be an ordeal. Reading doesn't have to be an ordeal. Those two beliefs make *HELP! For Parents* different from any parenting book you have ever read.

During my years of working with troubled parents and their troubled children, I have learned that all parents have problems with their children. Small problems will always be a part of parenthood. The danger is that little problems can grow into big problems, and big problems take all the fun from family life.

But I have also found that many problems can be avoided, and existing problems can be solved, once parents understand their job as parents. Beyond everything else, parents are teachers! Children have to learn how to live, and during their early years, up to age twelve, they learn more from their parents than from any other source.

In language you can understand and use, this book gives you all the tools you will need to build your family into whatever you want it to be. Once you learn how to control what you teach, you can teach your children anything you want them to learn. And once you teach them to take care of themselves and to solve their own problems, you will find that joy and love will resume their rightful roles in your home.

1

Beyond Tomorrow

n old farmer told me about a young rabbit he once captured and took home for his daughter to raise. She was already raising two puppies—cocker spaniels I think he said they were.

"That crazy rabbit got to where it slept with those dogs," he said, "and ate with them and chased around the yard with them until pretty soon it forgot it was a rabbit and started thinkin' it was a dog."

Then he stopped talking and gazed at the horizon with eyes that had lost their sparkle, as if he were looking back across the years at some sad and painful event. But he had caught my interest, so I had to interrupt his memories.

"Well, what happened to the rabbit?" I asked.

"Had to shoot it," he said. "It went bad and started killin' chickens."

There are two morals to that story. First, you can't believe everything you hear. Second, and more to the point, if you raise a rabbit to think it's a dog, then don't be surprised when it prefers Alpo to clover.

What does that have to do with raising children? Almost everything, because the same principle applies. If your children learn to think of themselves as dogs, then they are going to live dogs' lives. But if they learn that they are responsible, successful human beings, they will live successful, responsible lives.

This book is designed to help you teach your children only those things you want them to learn. They can learn to respect you and to respect themselves. They can learn to do better in school, to help around the house, to be happy, to be responsible. They can learn anything you want to teach them, once you learn to control what you teach.

What the Doctor Forgot to Tell You

"Good news—you are going to be a parent," the doctor said, and your life was changed forever.

Your doctor misled you with that smile and those words of congratulations. Little bundles of joy can grow into unbearable burdens of grief, but doctors don't tell you that. They never mention that your innocent infant will be among the most self-centered, helpless, annoying creatures ever to howl away the early morning quiet. They don't warn you that when morning sickness finally ends, heartsick days and sleepness nights have just begun.

There are better moments, of course. But there are many more bad times than you expected. Diapers and two o'clock feedings and noise—it seems endless, but it will change. From the moment of his birth, Junior is growing and learning.

He learns to talk. That will be useful later on when he wants to complain and sass and lie and swear. He learns to control his hands, which will come in handy when he wants to hit his sister or throw a rock through the neighbor's window. He learns to walk, then to run, and you begin to wonder if you will ever be able to keep up with him again.

There are better moments, of course, but when bad times get started, you think they will last forever. Kids are such a bother. They bring more grief and pain than any parent should have to handle. One of the great mysteries of human life is why anybody would want to have children at all.

The only answer is that children also bring the greatest joy and satisfaction you will ever know. That mixture of sunshine and thunder, of agony and ecstasy, of good times and bad—it's called life. As a parent, you are going to get both the bad and the good.

I can't tell you how to skip over the bad times and go straight to the good. The best I can offer is the chance for you to take more control and tip the scales a little, so life as a parent will bring you more joy and less sorrow.

You will learn to solve one problem, only to find others scratching at your door. But as you become a better teacher, and as your children learn to take responsibility for their own behavior, you will discover your problems growing smaller and easier to tame.

Every Parent's Got Them

Sometimes I think parents come to my office to deny they are having problems with their children.

"He's not really so bad," they will say about the son who is out of control. "I'm not sure why I'm here."

"You're here because Thomas is driving you absolutely crazy," I say.

"Well, yeah, I guess so."

"That's normal, you know."

"It is?"

"Do you know any parents who *don't* have problems with their children?"

"Well, the Johnsons don't seem to have any trouble. I watch them trooping merrily off to church on Sunday, and their kids seem so good, so perfect. One of these morning I'm going to turn the hose on them."

"The Johnsons have problems."

"Do you know them?"

"No. But I do know that all parents have problems with their children. Psychologists have trouble raising children. Ministers have trouble. Rich folk, poor folk, Republicans and lawyers and medicine men—every parent has problems with children. Even your neighbors, the Johnsons."

Children cause problems. They wet beds. They track mud across the carpet. They flunk. They fight. They spill. They smoke. They take drugs. They do almost everything adults do, and some things adults wouldn't think of doing.

Sometimes problems come from deep inside. Children may be born with faulty wiring or chemical imbalances or inherited tendencies toward certain destructive behavior. Sometimes children learn destructive behavior from someone else.

Whatever the cause, it all adds up to the same thing. There is a parent with an unhappy child, and a child with an unhappy parent. But no matter what causes problems, the solution is about the same. Children can learn better ways to live, and their parents can learn better ways to teach.

People are meant to be people, not to be perfect. They make mistakes as they live and learn. Problems will always be a part of being human. But improvement is possible, and learning is the key to improvement.

Good Things Happen

"Patty's grades are terrible, and she doesn't seem to care. What can I do?"

"What have you done?"

"You name it. We've punished her and grounded her and taken her bicycle away, but her grades are worse than ever."

"You've been busy teaching her that bad things happen to children who do poorly. But have you taught her what happens when she does well?"

"What do you mean?"

"Patty is going to do better when *she* chooses to do better—not when you decide she needs to do better, and not when I decide she needs to do better, but when she decides to do better. So the best thing you can do is help her decide by showing her that good things happen to kids who do well."

A critical approach can't be trusted to improve behavior. It tears down the child who needs to be built up. It confuses children. It makes them feel bad, and they can't do their best when they feel bad.

All their lives, your children will find people eager to tell them what they have done wrong. But the people they want to listen to are the people who tell them what they do right. This book will help you be one of those people.

The techniques I describe are going to give you the control to solve problem behavior and replace it with the kind of behavior you want. You can teach your children to comply with your wishes. You can teach them to live happy, useful lives. But best of all, you can teach them that they are responsible for their own behavior.

Responsible Living

Let's start fresh. We'll create a new child—a bouncing, burping baby boy. We'll name him Bill.

Bill isn't much different from any other infant. He's good looking, of course, but all babies are beautiful. He has talents of his own, but it's too soon to know what they are. He does have potential, we can be sure of that. Potential means that he will find things he can do well, if we don't put too many barriers in his way.

Our job, since we created this child, is to give him a good shot at life. What can we teach him to help him grow into a reasonably happy, responsible adult? Is there one thing he can learn which will allow him to get what he wants out of life? I think there is. I think Bill needs to learn that he is responsible for himself.

It won't be long before infant Bill starts making obvious choices. He will choose between toys. He will begin to prefer some foods over others. He will choose whether to smile or scream.

As he grows, his range of possible choices will grow with him. He will choose his friends. He will choose which shirt to wear. He will choose how much effort he's going to put into his schoolwork.

Of course it would be simpler if we, with our greater wisdom and experience, chose for him. Then his socks would always match, his playmates would be good kids, he would respect his elders and eat right and look both ways before he crossed the street.

But we would find, as we tried to make all of Bill's choices for him, that he is still choosing. He is choosing whether or not to like the food we try to make him eat and the friends we try to make him tolerate.

He is deciding whether his schoolwork is his problem or our problem. He is deciding whether his well-being is his responsibility or ours. And finally, he is deciding how much trouble he is going to cause us.

Maybe we should accept the fact that Bill will always have his choice. Instead of choosing for him, let's teach him how to choose.

With our greater wisdom and experience, we can let him choose but still control his choices. He can choose to keep his room neat or let his toys and clothes fall where they may. He can choose to watch TV or do his schoolwork. But, by making sure that good things happen when he does well, we can guarantee that his choices will come to agree with ours.

We aren't going to criticize him, because we know that criticism doesn't help. Besides, whatever he does is his choice, and he is going to have to live with the consequences. If he doesn't want to eat his dinner, it's his stomach that is going to stay empty until breakfast, not ours. He can't help but learn that what he does has a direct effect on what happens to him. And that is how responsible living begins.

Whether or not Bill knows it, whether or not he even believes it, what he gets out of life is going to be just about what he deserves. Bill will learn many things in the years ahead, but nothing more useful than this: People get what they earn. When he learns that, he will begin choosing today's behavior according to what he wants for tomorrow. He will begin to live responsibly.

Beyond Tomorrow

Tomorrow is easy.

You will need to get cornflakes for breakfast. Susan will want a clean dress and socks. Tom needs to practice his spelling. Marsha has a book due at the library. There's soccer practice at three, a dentist appointment at four fifteen, a PTA meeting at seven.

No matter how hectic it may seem at times, most parents have learned to cope with one tomorrow after another. But what comes after tomorrow? What do you want your daughter to be five years from now? How will she like school when she's fifteen? Will she go on to college? What kind of job would you like her to have?

One day soon, Marsha is going to start living like an adult, with a job and a mate and children of her own. She will have grown some and learned some, but she will be the same person she is now. Everything she is as a child will be part of what she becomes as an adult.

Whatever problems Marsha has today can be fixed. I can show you how to solve most of them within a few days. But this is more than just a problem-solving book. This is a building book. As you shop for tomorrow's breakfast cereal and keep the dressers full of clean laundry, you are doing more than just raising a child—you are building that child into the adult she will become.

As you look beyond tomorrow, you begin to see that your child will need to know how to solve her own problems. She will need to know how to get what she wants. She will need to know how to take care of herself. She will need to know that she is responsible for herself.

That's a lot to learn. Some people never do, and they live troubled lives without ever suspecting that they cause most of their own misery.

In the pages ahead, you will discover how you can teach your children to take care of themselves. Nothing they will ever learn—not how to tie a shoelace, not how to read a book, not how to drive a car or fix a dinner—nothing will ever be more important than that.

2

Ready or Not

Ready or Not

A frantic mother called my office one morning and demanded an appointment. "It's an emergency," she said. "I've got to come in today!"

I had appointments all day, but since it was an emergency, I agreed to give up my lunch to see her.

At noon, Mrs. Johnson bustled into my office, dragging her five-year-old son behind her.

"What's the emergency?" I asked as they sat down.

"Look at him!" She pointed at her son.

I looked, and he smiled and waved.

"He's the emergency?" I was starting to wonder if I still had time to grab a sandwich.

"He can't read!"

"What?"

"My neighbor told me this morning that her three-year-old was reading already. Michael's five and can't read a lick. Watch!" She grabbed a journal from my bookcase and handed it to the boy. She was right. He couldn't read one word.

For this I skipped lunch? But I took a deep breath, ignored my growling stomach, and gave Mrs. Johnson her hour.

I explained that most five-year-olds don't read. I

showed her how unfair it was to Michael to compare him to the genius next door. I told her that she could help Michael get ready to learn to read, but there was no way he was going to start reading until he was ready.

What I was really telling her was, when you've seen one child, you've seen *only* one child.

When You've Seen One Child

Look at your child and say to yourself, "They don't make 'em like that anymore."

No other child in all the world is exactly like yours. Those hands are like no others. Those ears, those legs, that nose—never have parts like those been put together in just that way. Some parents with no understanding of self-image might tease a child about his looks, but they don't blame the child. I've never known a parent to say, "Why don't you have blond hair like Lisa does? How come your eyes aren't blue instead of brown?"

But parents sometimes say things like, "Why can't you get good grades like Brad does? How come you can't read as well as your little brother does?" It's easy for parents to see that children are different on the outside. It's not always so easy to accept that they are also different on the inside.

Traffic Jams

Unless there are problems with the body or the brain, every child eventually learns to walk. Every child learns to talk and ride a bike and use the toilet. But children have to move at their own pace. They never progress until they are ready, and there's nothing you or I can do to change that fact.

It takes me half an hour to drive home from work, except when the traffic is heavy. Then it takes me forty-five minutes, unless I have to detour around road construction. Then it takes me an hour. I can't cut the distance, and they're not likely to increase the speed limit, so it's going to take me at least half an hour to drive home. The only effect anyone can have on my time is to slow me down.

The same is true when children are learning something new. Michael has some distance to go before he can read a book. No matter what you do, it's going to take him a certain amount of time to get there. With your help and encouragement, he will arrive on his own schedule. There are a few things you can do to help him get started. There are many things you can do to slow him down.

When he is criticized, he builds mental road blocks that slow him down. When you compare him to faster kids, you damage his self-confidence and slow him down. He may still learn to read, but he will feel like I do after fighting traffic for an hour—tired and frustrated and not eager to start another trip.

Instead of worrying about what other kids are doing, praise Michael for what he has already accomplished and nudge him back on course when he strays. If you watch his progress with a positive outlook, he will go as far as he can, as quickly as he can, and arrive fresh and strong.

The Positive Approach

You are already expert at using the positive approach. Remember when your child was learning to walk? Those first steps out from the coffee table were a wobbly adventure. Was it a failure because it only lasted for five seconds? When the child fell, did you say, "Is that the best you can do? How come you only took two steps?"

No, like every parent has ever done, you applauded the attempt. You hugged the child. You wished you had had the movie camera ready. You called your friends and bragged a little. But when your child finally learned to walk and moved on to other pursuits, did you put the positive approach away and forget about it?

The same approach that helped Eric learn to walk will work as well when he learns to read, or to wash the dishes, or to get along with his sister. His first steps toward any new accomplishment are going to be just as wobbly as those first steps across the carpet. If you watch for him to fail and then criticize him, how eager is he going to be to try again? But if you watch for success and praise him, he will climb to his feet and take another step.

When we expect children to do their best, we might find it easy to be critical. They won't always measure up to the standards we set for them. If we expect them to beat some other child's best, there's no doubt we are going to cause problems. They have only their own abilities to work with.

But if we expect them to try—when they are ready to try—then we have found the key to the positive approach. The success is in the attempt. Children who are willing to try, then to pick themselves up and try again, are going to get somewhere.

When we applaud children for trying, they will try again. When we criticize them because they weren't quite good enough, they will be afraid to fail, so they will be afraid to try.

When Push Comes to Shove

Set four-year-old Becky in a swing and not much is going to happen. She will kick her legs and start the swing rocking, but she's not really going to move until she is pushed.

So you give her a push and she starts to swing. Push harder and she goes higher, laughing and yelling and begging for more. But if you push too hard, she crashes, and suddenly it's not much fun anymore.

The same thing will happen when she begins to learn a new skill, like reading. The first gentle push, the one that starts her moving, is called exposure. As a two-year-old sitting comfortably in your lap, she discovers books long before she can read them. When she is ready to start reading, books will be familiar to her, so she's already moving.

Soon she will be ready to move a little faster, and you can push her along by rewarding her progress. I will discuss rewards in later chapters.

But if her progress stops, if she gets bored or frustrated, or if you get frustrated or angry, you are pushing too hard and it's time to back off. Let her choose another book from the library. Let her succeed at something she's already done. Let her succeed, let her know she has succeeded, and she will work for more success.

Success plus success equals SUCCESS. It's the little successes that add up to a big success. First Becky learns to hold a book right side up. Then she recognizes a letter, then a word, and soon she's moving right along.

Exposure

"Jimmy's having trouble getting along in first grade," his mother tells me. "He doesn't like to read, and he doesn't like the other kids."

"What does he do at home?"

"All he wants to do is lie on the couch and watch TV."

"How many books does he have?"

"Well, we're waiting until he learns to read before we spend money on books."

"Does he have friends?"

"There aren't really too many other kids around our neighborhood for him to play with."

"What else is there for him to like but TV?" Kids who have never tasted books don't like books. Kids who have never played with other kids have trouble getting along with other kids.

New ideas are like new clothes. Your child has to try them on before you can know if they fit. If Jimmy's new T shirt covers his knees, it doesn't mean there is anything wrong with the shirt, and it doesn't mean there is anything wrong with Jimmy. He just needs a chance to grow into the shirt.

If a new skill or idea seems too big for Jimmy to handle, it doesn't mean there is anything wrong with the idea, and it doesn't mean there is anything wrong with the child. Jimmy just needs the chance to grow into it. But kids grow fast. If you wait too long between fittings, he may never get to wear the shirt, and he may never be comfortable with the idea or master the skill.

Great Expectations

With the new prisoner standing before him, the warden studied the man's long police record and shook his head. "I'm sure glad I didn't disappoint my folks like you disappointed yours."

"I didn't disappoint my parents," the young man said. "Since I was five they've been telling me I'd end up in prison someday."

When it comes to predicting a child's future, parents are almost always right. If you expect too little, that's what you will get. If you expect too much—well, parents seldom expect too much of a child. They just expect it too soon.

Life is a marathon, not a sprint. The fastest starter isn't always ahead at the finish line. That five-year-old in my office was in no hurry to get started reading. If his mother pushes him too hard too soon, she might push him right off the course, and then it will take more than one lunch hour to set him right.

But if she uses equal measures of patience and praise, and if she feeds him new ideas and new skills with a spoon instead of with a shovel, he will eventually run far enough to meet her greatest expectations.

3

One Step at a Time

One Step at a Time

I skipped the third grade. Now I don't say that to impress anybody—in truth, it wasn't because I was a brilliant student, but because I was the only third grader in my one-room school.

I remember Miss Swanson, my teacher, saying, "Tony, you did okay in second grade—why don't we just move you ahead to fourth?" But third grade was the year she taught basic math, and I never did pick it up. Somehow I managed to muddle through elementary school, then high school, then most of college, always trying to avoid classes that required math.

Finally my mathless past caught up to me. For a degree in psychology, I needed to take statistics, and statistics without math is like aspirin without water—it's tough to get down, and sure to leave a nasty taste.

So what did I do? I started *right where I was* and proceeded *one step at a time* until I got to where I needed to be. I found a third-grade math book, read every page and worked every problem, until I'd learned it. Then I got a fourth-grade book and read every page and worked every problem until I had *it* down. Then I did fifth grade, then sixth, one year at a time, on through high school and into college. By the time I finished, I not only passed statistics, but I had the highest grade in the class.

When applied to human behavior, this step-by-step approach is called "Shaping." Parents need to remember that *all* learning and *all* progress is made one small step at a time. If you expect Linda to read *War and Peace* before she can handle *Dick and Jane*, or if you think Paul will clean his whole room before he learns to put one book away, then you may as well expect your children to jump to the moon, for all the success you are going to have.

Giant Leaps

Human progress, because it is a series of tiny advances, is seldom dramatic. When it seems a great leap has been made, when a man takes those first jubilant steps on the moon, the breakthrough astounds us primarily because we notice only the "giant leap for mankind" and not the countless small steps that lead up to it.

Any rational person who lived in any age before ours knew that it was impossible for a human to leave a footprint, not to mention a used car, on the surface of the moon. If we can see farther and reach higher today than our great grandparents could, it is only because we are standing on their shoulders, adding what we learn to all that was learned before we came along. It's called progress. Whether it is made by a planet or a nation or an individual, progress means building, piece by piece, on top of what is already there.

Step by Step

I couldn't build a rocket and get it to the moon. That's not my field. But I can do something which may amaze you even more—I can teach you how to get Mary to keep her room clean. As down-to-earth as that may seem, it requires the same step-by-step approach that put the first footprint on the moon.

Step 1.

Decide exactly where Mary is right now with her room cleaning, and decide exactly where you want her to be: "Right now, it's a miracle if she kicks a dirty sock toward the door. I would like her to make her bed every morning, put away her toys and books and dirty clothes, and make sure her entire room is clean and tidy."

Step 2.

Break the goal (a clean room) into as many smaller, more specific goals as you can, and list them in the order you want them accomplished:

1. Make bed.
2. Pick up dirty clothes.
3. Put books away.
4. Put toys away.
5. etc.

Step 3.

Start working on *only* the first step, making the bed. Now it is time to stop all your criticism of how the bedroom looks. Instead, start watching for anything that resembles bed-making, and praise and reward it: "Mary, I appreciate the way you straightened your sheet this morning—here's a quarter for your good work."

Never mind that the straightened sheet was an accident—she probably pulled it up while she was searching for a lost cookie or something. If you want to encourage her sheet-straightening, reward it.

When parents reward behavior with approval or praise, the child feels good and the behavior is likely to continue. When behavior is rewarded with a material reward, it is branded into the child's memory, and it will continue. When they are used together, these two kinds of rewards are a parent's most powerful tool for establishing desirable behavior. In later chapters, I will discuss rewards in more detail.

Step 4.

Reward her each day she straightens the sheet. She has been allowed to choose the first step in her bedmaking, even if it was an accident, but you want it to become established behavior, so reward it.

Step 5.

Reward her each time she takes a new step forward, and stop rewarding her for continuing the previous step. If she replaces the pillow, she has made progress and has earned another reward.

Step 6.

Continue this program until that glorious morning when Mary actually makes her bed. Then throw a party. Call Grandma and brag. Make Mary your Queen for a Day. Then sustain her behavior with occasional praise, and start working on the next small step toward a clean room, using exactly the same techniques you used to get the bed made.

The Gunnysack Approach

Last week Dan's parents brought him in to see me. "He hits his sister, wets his bed, flunks school, lights fires in the laundry room, steal hubcaps, smokes pot, and won't wash the dishes," they told me. "Would you please fix him by this weekend—we're having company."

Like many parents I see, they expected just a little more than a miracle. Trudging into my office with a gunnysack full of troubles on their shoulders, they emptied it onto my desk, giving it a good shake to be sure I got the whole load.

"Here you go!" they seemed to be saying. "Just make sure we don't leave here with any of the garbage we brought with us."

We sat there for a moment, staring at each other across the pile, all of us feeling hopeless and helpless and overwhelmed. Then I caught my breath and, sorting through the mess, chose one of the problems.

"You say he wets his bed? Let's start with that. How would it be if we help him stay dry tomorrow night?"

I wasn't going to solve all Dan's problems at once. I wasn't even trying to cure his bedwetting. I only expected a slight improvement—just one night with dry sheets. But his parents felt better immediately.

When you feel hopeless and helpless and overwhelmed, it is either because you think the job is too big for you, or you don't know where to start. I gave Dan's parents a place to start, with a goal they could handle, and their hopeless, helpless, overwhelmed attitude began to change. Suddenly they had hope and energy again, and they were eager to get started.

A bricklayer doesn't build a wall. He just lays one brick. Then he lays another next to it, then another, and another until eventually, by laying brick next to brick and row on top of row, he has his wall. Big walls don't necessarily demand larger bricks than small walls do, just more bricks. Big accomplishments don't necessarily demand larger steps than small accomplishments do, just more steps.

You can't instantly rebuild your child. You can only establish one small piece of behavior or eliminate another. But if you do that over and over, piece by piece, letting success build on top of success, you will eventually shape your child into a happy, responsible adult.

4

I Told You So!

I Told You So!

uzy Jones was eight when her mother brought her into my office. "Ever since she was born, Suzy's been the clumsiest kid in the world," Mrs. Jones said.

It's not often I meet someone with world standing, so I looked closely at the girl. She looked all right to me.

"You say she's had trouble since she was born?"

"She tripped over a shadow the first time she tried to walk, and she's been tripping over shadows ever since."

"It's not all that unusual for toddlers to stumble," I said.

"Especially if they're clumsy."

Just then Suzy turned to say something to her mother and bumped a lamp with her elbow. It rocked back and forth for a moment, then crashed to the floor.

"See, I told you so!" Mrs. Jones looked almost happy.

"I told you so!" is one of the most powerful phrases a parent can say. But, like Mrs. Jones, many parents have it backwards.

When she said, "I told you so," Mrs. Jones thought she had predicted the future. What she had really done was create her daughter's future. Children try to be what they are expected to be. They tend to grow into their labels.

The Chains That Bind

To tame a young elephant, a trainer will chain it by one leg to a post. The animal will fight the chain, struggling to run free, sometimes until the shackles dig through its thick hide into the flesh. But eventually it decides the chain cannot be beaten and quits trying.

Then the trainer can take the chain from the post and the elephant will stand calmly. Although the other end is lying free, in the elephant's mind the chain around its leg is still holding it captive. It is bound by a mental chain, and mental chains are stronger than steel.

Mrs. Jones used the same technique to train her daughter to be clumsy. She helped Suzy build mental chains that would not let her run free. All children begin life as if they were shackled. They can't walk, they can't control their hands or their toes, they can't even lift their heads. But as they grow and practice, they master movement, and the chains snap away.

Every time Suzy tried to break loose, her mother reminded her that she was still tightly bound: "You spilled your milk, Clumsy. . . Get off the swing before you fall. . . Don't run—you'll trip and skin your knees again."

Soon Suzy had built unbreakable mental chains that would not let her escape her clumsiness. Mrs. ιes was right when she told me that she had a clumsy daughter. What she didn't have to tell me was that she had trained Suzy to be that way.

Focus

Last summer I bought one of those fancy cameras with several lenses and too many knobs. I read the instruction manual, figured out how to load the film, then marched the family out to the backyard so I could practice what I had learned.

It only took me ten minutes to shoot two rolls of film. It took the store a week to get my pictures back to me. Except for my wife and kids, the whole family was excited to see the results.

The pictures really weren't all that bad. In one, the kids are in focus but the apple tree behind them is just a green blob. In another, the tree is in focus but the kids are blurred. Studying those pictures, I learned something basic about photography—what you focus on is what you are going to see when the picture is developed.

You will discover that the same principle applies to child-raising. Whatever behavior you focus your attention on is the behavior you are going to see the most clearly as your children develop.

Make Suzy believe she is clumsy and she will be clumsy. Remind Bob that he is shy and he will be shy. Start noticing when Joe cleans his room and he will keep his room clean.

When you focus on any part of Tommy's behavior, you are giving him a picture of himself. It is through your eyes that he learns to see himself. The picture he develops in his mind is called his self-image. It will stay with him as he grows and will always be there to tell him what he is and what he can do.

Self-Image

When I was a child, my family shared a farmhouse with my uncle and his family. Cousin Joe and I were always together, through good times and bad. Unfortunately, our good times often meant bad times for our parents.

Once Betsy, our best milk cow, dried up, and Uncle Bill could find no other reason for it, so he decided Joe and I were somehow to blame. The next morning, when he should have been off working in the fields, he decided to play detective and spy on us from behind the barn.

I don't know when Uncle Bill saw us. We first saw him when we rode Betsy around the corner of the barn and he jumped out, a curse on his lips and murder on his mind. To Uncle Bill, riding cows was an unpardonable sin, because cows that are ridden quit giving milk.

We had learned to climb on Betsy's back and get her moving, but we never did learn to steer her. So when Uncle Bill jumped out in front of us and tried to grab Joe, old Betsy just trotted straight along, and Uncle Bill had to dive to one side to keep from being trampled.

Before he could pick himself up, I was off that cow and running for the barn. Joe was right behind me, but Uncle Bill was right behind Joe.

I got away and hid in the hayloft. Joe wasn't fast enough. Uncle Bill caught him, threw him to the floor, and whipped him hard enough and long enough for both of us.

When he had finally used up his rage, Uncle Bill stood panting over his sobbing son. Joe looked up at his father and said, "I'm just plain bad. You always tell me that. And Tony's always good. That what his father tells him. But the thing is, *we always do the same things*."

What a child learns to believe about himself is called his self-image. A healthy self-image is as important as a healthy heart or healthy legs, because it determines how well a person is going to live his life.

Joe and I are adults now, but we are no longer together. While I have raised my family and enjoyed my life, he has struggled. Now he is confined to a mental hospital. The difference was in our self-images.

I thought enough of myself to finish college and begin my career. Joe though too little of himself to try much of anything. I was a good boy, Joe was a bad boy, but we always did the same things.

What Will Johnny Say?

No matter what abilities or talents your child may have, anything you do to build that child's self-image will increase the chances of future success. Anything you do to destroy self-image will increase the chances of failure. A turtle with a good self-image is always going to get farther in life than a rabbit with a bad self-image.

When Johnny's parents look at his past failures and use them to predict future failures, they are teaching him to have a bad self-image. "What do you mean you want to be a heart surgeon? You got a D in math last year. You've got to be smart to be a doctor."

What will Johnny say to himself? "I'm too dumb to be a doctor."

When Nancy's parents look at past successes and use them to predict future successes, they are teaching good self-image. "You did well in first grade. I bet you are going to go to college someday."

What will Nancy say to herself? "I'm going to college someday."

Which child will go to college?

The Truth

Sometimes a parent will ask in amazement, "Are you telling me to ignore the truth?"

"No," I say. "I am telling you that you have created the truth, and you can change it."

The truth is, parents decide what to believe about their children.

"Tom is a mean kid," Mr. Thomas tells me.

"How do you know?"

"He hits his sister."

"And you let him know he's mean?"

"Sure I do. It's the truth."

Tom was three when he first hit his sister and learned the truth—he was a mean kid. And he believed it. Why should a three-year-old believe anything else?

What do mean kids do? They hit their sisters. So Tom hit his sister again, and was again reminded that he was a mean kid. Being mean became a part of what Tom knew he was. If he wasn't being mean, he wasn't being himself.

The truth was, Tom was a mean kid. The truth also was, even kids who aren't mean hit their sisters. Children may try anything as they learn how to live.

If Mr. Thomas had taken notice instead when Tom shared with his sister—"What a good brother you are!"—he would have created a different truth—"Tom is such a friendly kid."

Children have to learn how to behave. What they learn becomes part of them and dictates how they will behave in the future. The truth is, your son is not a bad boy until he learns that he is bad. Your daughter is not a good girl until she learns that she is good.

Before a cannery worker puts a label on a can, he finds out what's inside. Then he can choose the right label. But when parents put labels on children, they are using only one type of behavior to describe a child with almost unlimited potential. Change the label on a can and the beans inside will still be beans. But children grow to fit the labels they wear.

Someday, when your children are grown, you are going to be talking about them and say, "I told you so!" If you control what you tell them now, while you are still helping to create their futures, you will have the joy of saying, "I told you so—I always said she would finish college. I told you he would be a good father someday. I told you she was going to be happy when she grew up."

When you put a label on a child, you are placing an order for future behavior. You can use labels to chain them to their past failures, or you can use labels to help them slip out of their chains and move on to greater accomplishments. Whichever approach you choose, expect your order to be filled.

5

Tradition

I was still in college when our first child was born. For weeks I spent what little free time I had converting a spare bedroom into a nursery. I would study, then paint, and study, then scrub, and study, then hang curtains. Finally, and just in time, the room was as close to perfect as any newborn should expect. But my wife had one more project in mind.

"Now you can tack a blanket over the window," she said.

"What?"

"Take this blanket and tack it up to cover the window."

"That's about the silliest—I mean, why would I want to do that?"

"To keep out the light, I think. Anyway, that's what my mother always did."

"Call your mother and find out why."

She grumbled and grumped and argued, but she finally got her mother on the phone. "Mother doesn't know why," she reported as she hung up the phone. "She said that's what *her* mother always did."

"So call your grandma."

She griped and groaned, but at last she called Grandma.

"What did she say?" I asked when the conversation had ended. "Or was the answer buried with Great Grandma?"

"Grandma said that Grandpa wasn't much of a carpenter, but there was a pane broken from the nursery window. To keep out the summer bugs and the winter snow, he nailed a blanket over the window."

Most of what we know about raising children is traditional, taught by one generation to the next until we begin to believe that Moses brought it down from the mountain with him, etched in eternal stone. If your grandparents spanked your parents, your parents probably spanked you, you probably spank your kids, and they are probably going to spank your grandchildren. That's a lot of spanking, without anybody ever stopping to ask if spanking is really the best thing to do.

Some of your family traditions contribute to your child's self-esteem, teach responsibility, and remind you that you are a family. Keep those traditions polished and on display, because they are family treasures. But others may work to destroy a child's self-image, or teach things you don't want your child to learn. Dump them and replace them with something valuable. Why carry that kind of garbage through life when you can exchange it for treasure?

Garbage

"This garbage has been in our family for years," some parents seem to tell me. "Now I want to pass it along to my children."

Criticism, negative attitudes, child abuse, drug abuse—the garbage I see in a week would fill a dumpster. If you find the solutions to your problems at the bottom of a liquor bottle, then that's where your children will look for their solutions. If you criticize, your children will be critical. It's by watching adults that children learn how to live. Like it or not, you are being watched.

One afternoon Mrs. Smith came charging into my office, stabbing the air ahead of her with a burning cigarette and dragging her daughter along behind.

"This is Ashley," she said, nodding at the girl as they sat down. "She's been smoking and drinking and cutting school." I handed Mrs. Smith an ashtray.

"Where do you think she learned to smoke?" I asked.

"From her friends, I guess." She crushed out her cigarette and lit another.

"Tell me about your husband."

"You don't want to know about that bum. He drives a truck all week, and when he's home he's so drunk he can't tie his own shoelaces."

"Do you work."

"No—I used to, but it was too much hassle, so I quit. Now I draw disability from the state."

"So why are you here?"

It was a struggle for her, but Mrs. Smith tried to be patient. "We're here because Ashley has been smoking and drinking and cutting school."

"Kids almost always do what their parents do. Why should Ashley be any different?" Mrs. Smith was lighting her third cigarette, and I thought she was going to choke.

"Do you know that if both parents smoke, there is a very good chance that a child will grow up to be a smoker? If one parent smokes, the chances drop, but are still great that the child will smoke. But if neither parent smokes, the odds that the child will smoke drop to almost nothing.

"For twelve years you have shown Ashley that it's all right to smoke and drink. You have shown her that when the going gets tough, it's time to quit going. Now what do you think I can say to overcome your example?"

Responsible parents see themselves reflected in their children. They know that child abusers raise child abusers, and that drug abusers—even those with legal prescriptions—raise drug abusers. They also know that college graduates raise college graduates. One of the hardest things about being a parent is making yourself into the kind of person you want your child to become.

Television

My generation has seen the growth of a new tradition—television. As traditions go, TV watching isn't the worst. But which prime-time character would you choose as a model for your kids?

A television set is broadcasting into the average American home for over seven hours every day. If you are devoutly religious, your children may spend as many as seven hours each week in church. From age six, they spend thirty hours a week in school, nine months of the year. But the average child has access to television for fifty hours every week, fifty-two weeks every year. Have you ever wondered who's teaching those kids how to live?

What does television teach your child? Violence, deceit, trivial thinking, irresponsibility. And the stuff in between the commercials isn't much better.

What is television teaching your child? That life

is a spectator sport. That problems should be solved in an hour or less. That good news is no news, and only tragedy and failure are important.

What does television teach your child? That you can drink like a camel, drive like a moron, and jump from bed to bed without ever having to rock a cradle, because somehow it's all going to work itself out before the last station break.

If television is one of your family traditions, it could be time for a break. Soak up the silence for a moment. Then use the time to create or polish your own family treasures.

Family Treasure

Like you, I sometimes wish I belonged to a rich family. If only Grandfather had drilled for oil instead of planting corn, my life would have been so much better and easier—or would it? He built no fortune, but Grandfather did build a strong family, and that is an inheritance I can pass along to my children.

Howard Hughes had it all, everything but a family, so he had nothing—no apparent joy, no love, no tradition. Even the few relatives who emerged after his death to squabble over his dollars seemed distant, far distant.

The most valuable family fortune has no dollar value. It grows when it is shared. There is plenty for everyone, even when it is passed from generation to generation. The real treasure in any family is the family itself.

You are one link in a family chain, joined to your parents on one side and your children on the other. If the links are strong, the chain can be twisted and dragged in any direction but still remain intact. But if the links are allowed to corrode, the chain will lose its strength and the family will pull apart.

I see all kinds of kids with all kinds of problems, but the most troubled are those who don't belong to a family, so they don't belong anywhere. Many are being raised by a single parent. Single parents need to work twice as hard at building a sense of family by building strong traditions.

Without traditions, a family is only a bunch of people with the same last name. They have little else in common. But when traditions are shared, people begin to get a feeling of belonging.

Besides the personal stability that comes with family membership, traditions give kids a chance to absorb what the family has learned through the generations. Some of that knowledge might be better left behind, but most of it—ethical and moral beliefs, attitudes toward education and achievement, successful ways to deal with other people—can be the basis for strong and useful lives.

Your family is a treasure that needs attention. If you had a bag of gold nuggets, you would see to it that the seams and fabric in that bag were in good repair. But your family is worth more than gold, and the traditions that hold it together deserve the best care you can give them.

Building Traditions

As we build traditions, what we really want to do is build memories. We don't know exactly what will trigger a memory. But you have probably heard of Pavlov, the Russian scientist who rang a bell every time he fed his dogs. After a time, the dogs would hear the bell and salivate at the memory of past meals, even when no food appeared.

If Pavlov could trigger memories in a dog, surely we can teach our children to respond to our traditions. One secret is repetition—make every Thanksgiving or Hanukkah or Christmas a special family time, and your children will learn to associate holidays with good family feelings.

Birthdays are especially important, one day each year for a child to stand up and shout, "Hey! Look at me—I'm getting bigger and better, and I'm special." Our holidays are already in place, but we need to use them to pull our families together.

Take family vacations! Put the kids in the back seat of the family jalopy, the suitcases in the trunk, the dog in a kennel, and drive away from the everyday things that tend to pull the family apart. Explore new frontiers, or make a tradition of returning to the same spot each year.

The important thing is that the family is together as a unit. Unit means "one." Different people, but one family, eating together, playing together, relaxing together. Maybe even fighting together over a comic book or the choice of a restaurant, but at least you are together, not off to your different offices and classrooms.

Dust off the camera and take some pictures. Sometimes I ask my clients to bring in their family photo albums. I've noticed that when a family hasn't been doing well, there will be a gap in the album. It is the good times that we all want to preserve and remember, and pictures are the best way I know to keep good memories in focus and in circulation.

Everyday Traditions

Vacations and holidays are special times, but probably the most important traditions are those built around daily life. Take walks or play games after dinner. Eat picnics in the park on Sunday afternoons. Read together, learn together, live together. The key to family traditions is the word "together." Build togetherness, and from the cradle to the crematorium you and your children will know the strength that comes only from a family.

When life was slower, families used to eat every meal together. The dinner bell would sound and three or four generations would appear at the table. But now Jennifer has dance lessons, Dad is working late, Grandma is at her condo in Southern California, and we eat on the run. We've traded three generations worth of family for fast food to go. What we've gained in convenience we've lost in togetherness.

Make the special effort to build a tradition around mealtime, even if it's only one meal a week. Sunday morning pancakes or Saturday afternoon barbecues can help transform a group of close relatives into a close family.

Safe Trails

Nowadays I wear shoes and walk mostly on concrete or carpet. But I still remember my barefoot days as a child. Near the farmhouse where many people walked, the dust was always deep and safe for bare feet. But farther from home where the paths were rocky and less familiar, I had to watch my step.

Strong family traditions are like those paths closest to home, familiar trails that your children can follow in comfort. As they grow older and venture out to find the going a bit rockier, they will remember home as a place where they felt safe and strong. The strength will stay with them, the feeling of belonging will stay with them, and for the rest of their lives they will benefit from the treasure you have given them.

6

Life Maps

As the East High football team was dressing for the first game of the season, the coach walked into the locker room.

"This is a big game, but we can win if we throw enough passes," Coach Jones began.

"But Coach, we haven't practiced passing," the quarterback said nervously.

"That doesn't matter—you can handle it. Now you linemen, I need you to block hard on every play."

A big tackle looked up from his locker. "Hey Coach—what's a block? Did we practice that?"

"No, we didn't practice it, but it's easy. Just . . . I mean, all you have to do is . . . just block. Now if you running backs will hit the holes, we'll score some points. What is it son?" he asked his fastest runner, whose name he never could remember.

"What's a hole, Coach?"

"It's too late to worry about that. I really meant to teach you how to run and block and pass and tackle, but we spent so much time inflating footballs and fitting jerseys that I didn't get it done. So you boys just go out and do your best, and I hope you win."

How would you like to have your grocery money bet

on that team? How much are you willing to bet on your children if you don't prepare them for the game of adulthood before they begin to play?

What is Your Game Plan?

Like all coaches, parents must plan for success if they are going to field a team of winners. Childhood is practice for adulthood. The game your children are learning now is the same game they will play as adults. If kids don't learn to handle life while they are practicing, they are not going to perform well when the bands tune up and the scoreboard lights come on.

How can you prepare your players for the big game? First you need to decide what you want to teach them. How important is education? What should they learn about money, sex, responsibility, drugs, marriage? Do you want them to share your religious or political beliefs? What will you teach them now to give them a better shot at future success?

When I ask parents what they want for their children, I know it's not an easy question, but it needs to be answered. If you decide to leave your child's future to chance, chances are you will be troubled by the result.

Life Maps

Christopher Columbus meant to find a shortcut to India but found a new world instead. That sort of thing can happen to anyone—there's no telling what we will bump into when we sail off without a map.

I began my graduate work in psychology the same way Columbus began his voyage. I had an idea where I wanted to be, but wasn't sure how to get there without falling off the edge of the world.

I did have one advantage—I wasn't sailing into unmapped waters, because others had been where I wanted to go. I only needed to follow the same route they had taken.

So I drew myself a map—not a map of the world, but something better—a map of my life. World maps may help you change your location, but life maps can help you change your future.

My map was a stack of index cards. Using a college catalog, I wrote every class I needed on a separate card, then arranged them in the order I would take them. After I finished a class, I threw the card away. So long as I used my map, I stayed on course, and I knew, as the pile got smaller, that I was getting closer to my destination.

Many of the other students in my classes seemed to be drifting through their studies. Some drifted away from school altogether. The kids I see in my practice are drifting. Their parents are drifting. Drifting is what you do when you let the wind and the current decide your destination, instead of mapping your own course.

I Dunno

"What do you want to be when you grow up?" I asked Bill during our first session together.

"I dunno."

"You dunno?"

"Nope."

"What do you expect of Bill when he grows up?"

I asked his mother when she came in.

"I dunno."

"You dunno?"

"Nope."

Parents who don't know what kind of future they want for their children will raise children without much of a future.

Bill came back a week later, and I helped him start moving from "I dunno" to "I want to be."

"What do you *like* to do?" I asked him.

"I like to ride my horse."

"You like animals?"

"Yes."

"Would you like to be around animals when you grow up?"

"Sure."

"You could be an animal doctor, a veterinarian. Do you think you would like that?"

"That would be great."

"But you would have to start getting better grades in science—could you do that?"

"I guess so."

I didn't pull out an application for veterinarian school and have Bill start filling it out. He had been struggling with sixth grade, so he wasn't ready to worry about graduate school.

I just wanted to plant some ideas in his mind. He is going to grow up someday, and he is going to do something when he does. I will put no limits on what he can accomplish if he is willing to work hard enough and aim high enough.

As you begin to help your child shift from "I dunno" to "I want to be," the same method will work for you. Start with what your child already likes to do, and build it into a possible career. Don't worry about what *you* think your child can do. Assume that anything is possible, make it seem possible to your child, and suggest the first step that will lead toward the goal.

Later that same week I saw Joey and her mother. "What do you want to be when you grow up?" I asked Joey.

"An astronaut!"

"That's great. What will you need to do to become an astronaut?"

"I have to learn all about science and math."

"So you'll need to work hard in school and go on to college, won't you?"

"Yes, I will."

I am not saying that sixth graders need to make a final decision on a career. Many of today's children will end up with jobs that haven't been invented yet. But when children can say "I want to be," good things start to happen.

Since Joey realized that she could be something sometime, she knew that her work in school would affect her future. Success is success—the attitude that lets Joey do well in first grade is the same attitude that will let her do well in college and then help her land the job she wants, or land her on the moon. What she does today will determine what she can do tomorrow.

Learning to set goals teaches children that "when I'm grown up" is the time that is really coming, and a time that can be improved by planning. Children may not know that childhood doesn't last forever. Many children can't see ahead to the day when Mom and Dad won't be there to solve all their problems for them. But that day is coming. If it comes before your children are ready, what chance will they have?

Once children learn to choose their own routes, they will travel much farther and stumble less often.

Options

Two years ago Dr. Harris, a local heart surgeon, decided he needed to take time out from his practice. While he was in college he had worked summers as a bricklayer, so he called his old boss. The conversation went something like this:

"Bob? This is Tom Harris."

"So what's up, Doc?"

"I need a break from this pressure cooker, Bob, and I wondered if you could use a hand for the summer."

"You're kidding, right?"

"No, Bob, just tired."

"Well, one of my guys is going to quit this month. If you're sure you want it. . . ."

"I can start in two weeks. Thanks, Bob."

So Dr. Harris got his partners to take his cases and went off to lay brick for the summer.

The bricklayer he replaced was named Al. Al's father had laid brick, so had his grandfather, and from the day he was born everyone knew that Al was going to be a bricklayer. But after twenty years he was sick and tired, and he finally quit.

Al had always dreamed of being a doctor, so he went to visit a counselor at the university. The conversation went something like this:

"I want to be a doctor. What do I have to do?"

"How are your grades?"

"I did pretty good in junior high."

"I mean, how are your college grades? You need good grades in college to get into medical school."

"College? Well, after my sophomore year I quit high school and started working. But now I'm thirty-six years old, sick of bricklaying, and want to be a doctor. What should I do?"

"Lay brick."

It's easier for a doctor to lay a brick than for a bricklayer to mend a heart. Doctors have more options than bricklayers.

As you think about what you want your children to learn, you need to think about options. One of the hard facts of life is that people can do things to increase their options, or they can limit their future choices by what they decide today.

Education opens doors. Lack of education slams them shut. Positive attitudes help people approach their potentials. Negative attitudes hold them back. Good health increases the chance of success. Burdening the body with unnecessary drugs or unnecessary weight increases the chance of failure.

Climbing

The road to a successful life runs uphill. Some people choose small hills to climb, then waste a lifetime trying to find a shortcut to the top. Others look up at a distant peak and spend their days imagining how wonderful the view must be from the top.

But there are a few who actually climb to the clouds. They are the people who know how to plan. First they choose a mountain. Next they study it to decide their route. They might learn from those who have already been to the top. Then they begin to climb, one step at a time, until they are as high as they can go.

Mountains are tricky things. You never know when avalanches or rivers or grizzly bears are going to block your path. There are no guarantees that you will reach the summit, but the higher your goal, the higher you are likely to climb.

Life can be tricky. There are always roadblocks and ravines and dead ends. But the higher your goal, the more successful you are likely to be. And the sooner your children learn about working toward goals, the greater will be their chances of success.

Cattle Guards

Driving through the western United States, you are likely to see white lines painted across the road. They don't interfere with your progress. You won't even feel them beneath your tires. But the biggest, meanest bull on the range will not cross those painted lines, not even to escape the butcher.

To the bull, those white stripes mean danger. Ranchers often dig a pit in the road, then cross it with steel rails to allow passage to cars but uncertain footing to livestock. The cattle have learned about cattle guards, so now a painted cattle guard will work just as well as the real thing. A two-thousand-pound bull can be held back by an ounce of white paint.

Most of the barriers people erect for themselves and their children are even less real than a painted road. When we teach children to drift instead of to plan, we are limiting where they can go. When we teach negative attitudes and negative self-images, we are painting lines across roads our children could take. Like the bull at the edge of the road, they can be bound by their own imaginations, never daring to take the first step into another field.

But people who map their own lives don't see imaginary barriers. Instead, they are looking ahead, going where they need to go to get where they want to be, and they won't be trapped by lines painted across a road.

going where they need to go to get where they want to be, and they won't be trapped by lines painted across a road.

7

Warden or Teacher

Warden or Teacher

"Can I mow your lawn?" The young girl at my door was willing to work, but I wondered if the job wasn't bigger than she was.

"Why would you want to do that?" I asked.

"I need the money."

"You need the money?"

"I was playing ball in the living room, and I broke my mother's favorite lamp."

"Was she mad?"

"No, she just said I could earn enough to buy her another one. Can I mow your lawn?"

"Sure, you can mow my lawn."

I knew the family. Cathy's older brother was an A student all through high school and just that year had earned a university scholarship. Cathy's sister made the honor roll each term, and she was president of her junior class. Now here was Cathy, age eight, giving me a clue as to why success seems to run in that family.

Cathy's mother taught her children that they were responsible for their own behavior. She taught them that they could do whatever they wanted, as long as they were ready to clean up their own messes. And she found, as her children grew and her lessons took hold, that they made fewer and smaller messes.

Cathy's mother knew she was a teacher, so she was careful when she taught her children, and she taught them well.

The Warden

As Cathy began to push the mower across my yard, I compared her mother to another mother who had come to my office the day before.

The longer she was there, the more Mrs. Gardner reminded me of a prison warden. Never once did she take her eyes off the prisoner in her charge, who happened to be her eight-year-old daughter: "Don't scratch . . . sit up . . . speak clearly . . . sit still . . . ."

I couldn't imagine how Kerry had endured it for eight years, because five minutes was all I could stand. "She takes a lot of watching, doesn't she?" I asked.

"I have to watch her every second of the day."

"What happens if you don't?"

"She gets into some kind of trouble. Yesterday I let her go for ten minutes and she beat up the neighbor boy and took his bike. The day before that I turned my back and she destroyed my pansies. And just last week . . . ."

I interrupted: "So what's your job as a mother?"

"I have to keep her out of trouble."

"Does it work?"

"That's why I'm here. Any time I don't watch her, she's into some kind of mischief."

"I know. Escaped prisoners are not to be trusted."

When parents get the idea that children need to be watched constantly, they turn into wardens and turn their homes into prisons. Worse yet, they turn their children into prisoners.

Outside the Cell Block

Your job as a parent is *not* to keep your children out of trouble. Your job is to teach them to keep themselves out of trouble. That's the best news you've heard all day, because it releases you from an impossible task.

You can turn your home into a prison. You can treat your child as a prisoner who needs constant supervision. But who's going to climb into the guard tower when you aren't around?

When Kerry gets time off to go to school, who's going to supervise her behavior? Her teacher can't—schoolteachers are too busy to play warden. And Kerry can't watch herself. She's never learned how.

When Kerry has served her time at home and begins life as an adult, who's going to control her behavior? Her husband? That sounds like trouble for sure. And she still won't be able to take care of herself, because she's never learned how. Children who don't have the chance to be responsible for themselves won't have the chance to grow into responsible adults.

A parent who thinks like a warden tries to lock every door. "You can't be trusted, so I'm going to make sure you don't have the chance to go wrong," Mrs. Gardner told Kerry.

A parent who thinks like a teacher opens every door. "You can do whatever you want," Cathy's mother told her. "But whatever you do might affect the rest of your life. Let me help you learn to choose wisely."

Both of these parents are trying to control their children. The warden thinks control should come from outside the child. The teacher thinks control should come from inside. That difference makes all the difference.

Control

When it's time to stop your car, you usually have two choices. You can do it gently from the inside with the brakes, or you can wait for something outside the car—a tree or another car—to do it for you. Either way, your car will stop. But if you want to avoid damage or injury, choose the brakes instead of the tree.

When a child needs to stop, parents usually have two choices. They can trust him to control himself from the inside, or they can try to use some outside force—a spanking or scolding—to do the job.

Mrs. Gardner thought that if she erected enough barriers, she would keep Kerry from swerving off the straight and narrow. Unless something changes, by the time Kerry reaches adulthood her self-image will be bashed and battered from running headlong into those barriers. And she will have learned to be irresponsible, because she expects someone else to set her limits and control her behavior.

But teachers raise children who learn how to control themselves. Those kids know that what they do will determine what they get, so they do things that contribute to their own sense of worthiness—not because they have to, but because they choose to. And when they make a mistake or make a wrong turn, they know how to put on the brakes.

Whether you are trying to control a car or a child,

internal controls are alway more effective and less likely to cause damage or injury than outside controls.

A Warden Learns to be a Teacher

"So what do I do now?" Mrs. Gardner asked me. "I can't just turn her loose."

"No, you don't want to throw her overboard before she learns to swim. She has to learn responsibility one step at a time. Just watch for any responsible behavior, then reward it. You want to show her that responsibility helps her get the things she wants. And be sure she has the chance to be responsible."

"Like what?"

"Like ask her to be in charge of her own clothes, and reward any attempt she makes. You want to teach her that taking care of herself is her job, not yours. Don't forget that Kerry chooses her behavior, and you can't choose for her."

"Don't you think I should know what's best for my own daughter?"

"Probably, but that's not the question. The question is, how can you teach her to choose behavior that is constructive instead of destructive?"

"I don't know if I can teach her anything. She's stubborn as a mule."

"You've been trying to force the mule onto the road, but that doesn't work. It's so much easier to put a treat on the road, then wait for the mule to choose to go get it. That's what rewards do—make the behavior you want so attractive that your child will choose it for herself, without all the tugging and kicking and bellowing.

"You've built a prison around Kerry. You're right—you can't just turn her loose. But you can dismantle the prison, one block at a time, as you gradually teach her to handle the responsibility that comes with freedom."

Ideally, a parent would begin with an infant and guide her straight up the path that leads to responsible adulthood. But we are not ideal beings, so we have to start where we are and keep aiming at the place we'd like to be.

You are doing your child no favor when you decide you are going to force that child to behave. Using force won't work to control behavior. It won't prepare the child for adult life. And the life of a warden is not much fun for the parent, either.

The Prison Reunion

While they are on duty, wardens are held captive by the same system that turns their children into prisoners. Someone has to occupy the guard towers. Someone needs to be sure all the locks are locked and all the windows are barred. If the warden relaxes for a moment, one of the little desperadoes might escape, and there's bound to be trouble.

But eventually the prison empties. The children grow up and leave home. In fact, leaving home might sound so good to them that they won't wait to grow up before they leave.

With her children gone, the warden walks through her house and finds it quiet. The only footsteps she hears are her own, echoing from each abandoned cell. She has the joint to herself, whether she likes it or not. The life of an ex-warden can be a life of loneliness.

But one day the warden has an idea. "I know," she says to herself. "I'll have a reunion. A prison reunion."

So she sends out the announcements—to those inmates she can still locate. Then she gets ready for the big day, scraping the rust from the bars, oiling the locks, replacing the bulbs in the searchlights.

Imagine her surprise when nobody comes. But why should they? The emotional bonds between prisoners and their keepers are built on mistrust and resentment—emotions that repel rather than attract. And even if the children's damaged self-images have begun to mend, the memories of the bad times are better forgotten than relived.

And so we leave the warden—she who tried so hard to control her children but ended up with no control at all—alone in the prison she built, holding a reunion to which nobody comes.

Family Reunion

Although they are on duty, teachers enjoy the same amount of freedom they give their children. The responsibility is shared, the work is shared, so there is more time for everybody to share the good times. Family life is more fun when people learn to take care of themselves.

When her children grow up and start homes of their own, the teacher may be alone. She may even be lonely at times, but the strong bonds of love and respect she has built will keep working to draw the family back to her. Her children have homes where she is welcome, and she has a home where they can feel good about themselves, so the reunions are frequent and happy.

Then grandchildren come along, and the teacher's joy is multiplied as she sees her good teaching spread through her children to a new generation of responsible kids. Once again her halls are alive with the sound of children. She has been a responsible parent, and she will collect dividends for as long as she lives.

8

The Dragon Outside the Door

The Dragon Outside the Door

Mrs. Knight sat in one of my office chairs and stared at the carpet. Her husband sat next to her and studied the ceiling. I knew if we were going to talk, it was up to me to get things started.

"What's going on?" I asked.

Mrs. Knight was sobbing, so I turned to her husband. He shook his head, blinked his eyes, and spoke slowly:

"We're a religious family. We don't like swearing, we don't allow our children to swear, we don't even let them watch television shows if we think they will hear people swear. But last night at dinner Artie, our five-year-old, said, 'Pass the damn milk.' "

"He didn't even say please?" My little joke was wasted on the man, so I got serious. "Where do you think he learned that?"

"Well, he started at a preschool last week, and some of the children there might talk like that. We're careful when we choose his playmates, so I don't know where else he could have learned it."

"What did you do about it?"

"I jerked him from the table and dragged him to the bathroom and washed his mouth out with soap.

I don't think he's going to say that again."

The Knights had built a castle around their children to protect them from the evils that lurk out there in the real world. They believed that they had built strong enough walls and a deep enough moat to keep their home safe from invasion.

But then they allowed Artie to venture out, and a dragon had followed him home.

Some Facts About Dragons

Dragons are all those things you wish your children wouldn't learn. Children learn to swear. They learn to fight. They learn that there are things called drugs, and other names for potty, and how to try shifting responsibility by lying or making excuses.

Dragons are real. You may have convinced yourself that they are somebody else's problem, but the fact is that if you have children, the day will come when you meet your first dragon. You can be sure that many more will follow.

Dragons are plentiful. They are everywhere. Schoolyards are full of them. One may slide out of the television or spring across the hedge. If you watch out ahead, they sneak up from behind. If you look over your left shoulder, they come from the right. You can't avoid dragons.

Dragons can be powerful. They don't have to be—you can learn to rob them of their power. But until you do, they are hard to beat. Artie's father didn't understand dragons, so he went forth to do battle. Fighting dragons is a risky business.

Armed with a bar of soap, Mr. Knight attacked his dragon—a weakling, so far as dragons go, but still a dragon. To Artie, it was nothing. "Damn" was just one combination of letters that made no more sense to him than most other combinations. Imagine his surprise when his father treated that tadpole of a word like it was a real fire-breather.

The Drug Dragon

One morning last week, Mrs. Robins came to report a more dangerous dragon.

"Patti, my twelve-year-old daughter, was caught smoking marijuana with some other girls in the school restroom," she said.

"What did you do?"

"Well I told the little addict that she'd better never let me hear another word about her doing dope, or she'd be looking for another place to live."

"What else did you do?"

"We grounded her, of course. She has to come right home after school for the next month. And her father locked her bike up and threw away the key."

"Is that all?"

"Isn't that enough?"

"Sounds like plenty to me."

"What do you think I should have done."

"What can you do to change what's already happened?"

"Nothing."

"Then maybe that's the best thing to do. Doing nothing is always better than doing something to make the problem worse. If you wanted to punish her for her sins, it sounds like you did fine. But if you want to avoid future problems, you may need a different approach."

Drugs are one dragon that can threaten any family. Like every other child, yours is going to have the chance to try drugs somewhere along the line. Most kids are going to take the chance, at least once. And most of them will escape without hurting themselves. But some will have serious problems with drugs.

The drug dragon may seem more fearsome than other dragons, but it can be killed. And it can be killed with the same weapons that kill all the others.

The Life Cycle of a Dragon

So quietly that you don't even notice, a dragon is born as an idea in a child's mind. With its first breath, the dragon begins to whisper its little lies:

"There are easy ways to feel good. Get stoned. Get drunk.

"There are easier ways to handle school. Cheat. Don't go.

"You need to get back at your parents. Flunk math and watch Dad come unglued. Take drugs and watch Mom lose her mind.

"If you want to feel big, you need to smoke cigarettes or swear or do drugs.

"If you want other kids to like you, take drugs. Disrupt class. Have sex."

Dragons grow with attention. The more the whispers are heard and believed, the more powerful the dragon becomes.

Dragons die if they are ignored. A child who refuses to believe dragon lies is going to avoid a lot of serious trouble.

As a parent, you can do things to help the dragon die of neglect, or you can do things to feed the dragon and help it grow. Since you, from the outside, can't hear the dragons whispering to your child, you may be nourishing what you want to kill.

When you help children feel bad, they are going to listen more carefully when the dragon offers drugs or alcohol. When you give children the power to make you feel bad, they are more likely to embrace the dragon that offers them power.

But when you help children feel good about themselves, you are making the dragon's promises seem less appealing. A child with a good self-image doesn't need to take feelings of power or acceptance from dragons. A child with a good self-image doesn't need drugs to feel good, or cigarettes to feel big. A child with a good self-image is dragon-proof.

A violent attack may kill a dragon. But it may be just the food the dragon needs to grow. The deadliest weapon you have in your war on dragons is a shrug.

A shrug doesn't give power to the dragon, and it doesn't make the problem your problem. A shrug tells the child, "It's your life. You get to pick the tune, but you're the one who has to do the dance."

A shrug gives you time to rebuild your child's self-image, and that is the only way you are going to protect your child from other dragons.

Armor

Back in the misty days of yore, when men were men and dragons spit fire, people did not leave the castle without protection. They carried shields to deflect the dragon's scorching breath, and they wrapped themselves in armor to protect against the sharply pointed tail. That's the danger of dragons—they can get you coming or going.

So the dragon-fighters wore gloves and helmets and shoes, until every inch of skin was covered. Dragons were dangerous, and it was suicide to stand naked before one.

Things haven't changed that much. Dragons are still dangerous creatures. They can burn or stab or kill. And if we send our children out without protection, the dragons are going to get them.

The shield that will deflect a dragon's first thrust is a set of traditional values: People in our family do not smoke cigarettes. We are expected to tell the truth. We don't get high on drugs. We do well in school.

Holding such a shield before them, children won't let most dragons get near enough to do any damage. But to make a child completely dragon-proof, one more piece of armor is needed—a good self-image.

Children with poor self-images are bound for trouble. Those are the kids who flunk out or drop out or get stoned. They are the kids who lie and steal and fight and swear. A child with a poor self-image is dragon bait.

But take those children and rebuild their self-images, and suddenly they will be strong enough to withstand the fiercest dragon attack.

Dragons pick their victims. They know that kids who feel weak or unloved or unwanted are easy prey.

With so many dragons running around loose, a good self-image is a matter of survival. Anything a parent can do to build up a child is going to make that child's world a safer place. But any time a child is made to feel smaller and worth less, the world becomes more dangerous.

Living With Dragons

The Warrens looked like a typical family, except for one small thing. Candy, their twelve-year-old daughter, had pink hair.

"Look at her," Mrs. Warren demanded. "Isn't that the most disgusting thing you've ever seen?"

I shrugged and winked at Candy.

"She learned that from her big brother," the father told me. "She only does it to get me mad."

"Her brother's hair is pink?"

"No, purple. At least it was purple the last time I saw it."

"When was that?"

"Six months ago, when I told him to fix it or find another place to live."

"Does Candy have the same choice?"

"She has until Monday. Then she's out the door."

"You're going to run out of children eventually, aren't you?"

Parents don't have to approve of the choices their children make. Sometimes they will be disappointed or shocked or disgusted. But hair dye is temporary. Drug abuse can stop. School failure can be overcome.

Goodbye can be forever.

Life goes on, but goodbye may last for the rest of your life. Ten or twenty or fifty years from now you will still want your family to feel like a family. Which of these temporary problems is bad enough to make you want to give up those years of togetherness?

You can't fix what you can't reach. You may be disappointed in the choices your child makes, but if you want to have any influence on future choices, you might have to swallow hard and accept the child and the choice, even if it means allowing a dragon inside your castle.

9

Crime and Punishment

Not long ago a father marched into my office to complain about his son.

"I've beat that kid and beat that kid," he said, "but I can't get him to stop hitting his little brother."

If that father had taught his son to go to church, he would have expected to see him in church every Sunday. When he taught the boy to ride a bicycle, he was not surprised to see him pedaling down the sidewalk. But, by his own example, he had taught his son that hitting is the way to control someone smaller and weaker. And so he came to me, flabbergasted that his son had learned the lesson so well.

"Why do you hit your son?" I asked him. That's one of my favorite questions and, after years of asking, I think I've heard all the answers. I won't tell you which one that frustrated father gave, but there are really only five:

1. To make my kids stop doing what they are doing.
2. To teach my kids a lesson.
3. To relieve my own frustration.

4. Because my parents spanked me.
5. Because I don't know what else to do.

Whichever answer parents give, I'm ready for them. Here is my basic response to each of the five:

1) Yes, spanking does stop unwanted behavior, and it stops it immediately. In much the same way, a stick of dynamite stops weeds from growing in your flower garden, and it stops them immediately. But both solutions are only temporary, and both threaten the growth of something desirable—either a child's self-image or your prize petunias.

The way to raise a healthy garden is to make sure the flowers are well nourished and to remove the weeds without disturbing the petunias. It won't take too many dynamite blasts to convert your flower bed into a landscape suitable only for the weeds you were trying to destroy.

The way to raise a healthy child is to eliminate unwanted behavior without uprooting wanted behavior. A child's self-image is as impressionable as your well-prepared garden soil. Each spanking leaves a crater, and craters are better suited to weeds than to flowers. Unwanted, destructive behavior grows from a scarred self-image.

You may change behavior by spanking, but that is all you will do—change it. You probably won't improve it. Spanking does things to the child which ensure that unwanted behavior will continue.

2) Hitting children is probably the most effective way to teach them lessons. It teaches them to hit. It teaches them fear and anger and hatred.

What if the paddle were in another hand, and you

were the one being hit? Suppose you backed your car into another car, and the other driver jumped out in a rage, dragged you from your car, and began to beat you. Suppose he was three feet taller and ninety pounds heavier than you, so you were defenseless. How would you feel about that monster? Is that how you want your child to feel about you?

You can beat the lumps out of cake batter. You can beat the dirt from a rug. But when you try to beat the hell out of a child, you are creating your own little devil.

3) Hitting anything—a punching bag, a wall, a child—is an effective way to release frustration. But the punching bag did not cause the frustration. The wall is not responsible. The child just happens to be there. These are only targets for uncontrolled anger.

When children feel themselves losing control of their world, they scream and strike out. But no one pays them too much attention because they don't hurt anybody, so before long the anger is spent and the noise abates.

When parents lose control and strike out, children sometimes get in the way of the anger and get hit. Parental tantrums are really not much different from those thrown by a two-year-old, except parents have enough strength to be dangerous. Children are such easy targets. They can't hit back. They are almost always around. One name for it is "child abuse."

A battered child learns that the world is a dangerous, hostile place. Long after the bruises fade the child remembers how to be a victim.

4) You hit your children because your parents hit you? We have learned more about the dangers of corporal punishment than was known twenty or thirty years ago, and we have developed techniques that do the things spanking was supposed to do, without all the harmful side effects. Just as we rush to take advantage of new advances in medicine and transportation, we should welcome advances in the science of child-raising.

5) You don't know what else to do? I am ready to give you an alternative, now that I have shown why I believe corporal punishment causes many more problems that it solves.

Time Out

To eliminate unwanted behavior, you need to remember three things: 1) Behavior that is rewarded is repeated, 2) children are always learning, and parents are always teaching, and 3) traditional punishment *does not* eliminate unwanted behavior.

Combine those three principles into one workable system and you have Time Out. Time Out means "Time Out from reinforcement or rewards"—it does not reward unwanted behavior. And it is a tool that is used to teach, not punish. The most important thing that it teaches is responsibility.

After using Time Out on hundreds of kids, some of them even harder to handle than yours, I am ready to say that Time Out has only one flaw—the same flaw that is built into any tool. It only works right when it is used right. The best-designed, best-constructed, most perfectly balanced hammer in the world is no good until it hits the nail on the head. And Time Out won't do you any good until you learn when and where to use it.

The parent who bothers to use Time Out correctly

will see improved behavior within three days. I've used it with retarded kids and kids with severe learning disabilities—even with "normal" kids—and I know it always works to improve the behavior of any child from age two to puberty.

Time Out is basically the old sit-the-kid-in-the-corner routine, but with some very important refinements. Suppose that Mother has just asked young Michael to pick up his toys, but he chose to ignore her.

"Okay, Michael," she says, "you've earned Time Out." Michael already knows what that means—he will spend five minutes alone in the bathroom. If he resists, Mother calmly adds another minute, and continues to add minutes as long as the resistance continues.

When Michael starts serving Time Out, Mother places a portable timer outside the bathroom door, set for whatever time he has earned. When the timer rings, he emerges, and Mother repeats her request. Then Michael must decide whether he will comply and pick up his toys or start over with Time Out.

Don't be fooled by the simplicity of this system. The details that seem so small are what make Time Out work so well. If you want Time Out to work for you, you will have to follow these eight guidelines:

Use Time Out Only for Noncompliance

Time Out must be used following a reasonable request, one that Michael can satisfy if he chooses. When his mother asked him to put his toys away, the choice was his—either he picked them up, or he went to Time Out. He was learning responsibility because he had a choice, but also because he had to accept the consequences.

Use the Bathroom

The bathroom is the most boring room in the house. Five minutes alone there will seem endless to a child.

Parents often ask me why they can't just send Cathy to her room or make her sit in a corner. Those are not sufficiently boring places. Boredom equals lack of rewards, so it is boredom we want to cultivate with Time Out. Bedrooms are sanctuaries for toys and books and television sets, and a child sitting in the corner is the center of attention, especially when there are other children around. Attention is the most rewarding of rewards.

For the bathroom to work as a Time Out room, you will need to prepare it. Remove razor blades and medicines and your priceless antiques. Toys, books, and magazines will have to go. Beyond that, let children be responsible for themselves. If Michael chooses to flush a roll of Charmin down the toilet, he will replace it. If he makes a mess, he will clean it up.

I have studied video tapes of children in Time Out, and they are not violent or destructive. Usually they plop down on the toilet seat and sit there, so tense and angry you expect to see the room fill with steam. But five minutes is a long time for a child to stay angry, especially without an audience. When Time Out is over, they have relaxed and are calm and in control of themselves.

Keep Your Cool

If you allow your child's behavior to upset you, you are giving it power, and it will continue, whether you use Time Out or not. When you lose control of yourself you've lost control of your child.

The attitude that will make Time Out work for you is this: "My children's behavior is their responsibility, not mine. There is no reason for me to punish myself when they behave irresponsibly. My responsibility is only to teach them that they will get what they earn."

Do we get upset at a two-year-old when she mispronounces a word? No, because she is still learning to speak. Do we scream at a five-year-old who plays baseball in the living room? No, because he is still learning to act responsibly.

Use a Portable Timer

Let the bell tell the child when Time Out is over. If your child yells, "Can I come out now?" the timer just keeps on ticking. It doesn't have a headache or make exceptions or play favorites. It is perfectly happy to tick away the minutes and let the child on the other side of the bathroom door take responsibility for himself.

The timer must be portable so it can be placed where your child will hear it ring. Otherwise, you will be calling out, "Your time is up," and you become the one who releases the child. You want the child to understand that it was his behavior, not some whim of yours, that put him in Time Out, so let the timer release him while you stay out of it as much as possible.

If you will drive a small nail into the top of the doorframe, the timer can hang there permanently.

Explain Time Out Before You Use It

You want to teach your children that they are responsible for themselves, so they need to understand their choices. They can comply with a request, or they can serve Time Out. They can go to Time Out without stalling or complaining, or they can earn more time. They can wait for the timer to ring, or they can come out early and start over. They can comply with the original request after they serve Time Out, or they can return to Time Out.

Explain that you aren't going to hit them or yell at them anymore, because their behavior is their responsibility, not yours. The choice is simple—either they comply with a request, or they serve Time Out.

Don't Use Time Out With Traditional Punishment

Traditional punishment is not reliable, and if you combine it with Time Out, Time Out will not be reliable. When you spank children or yell at them before you send them to Time Out, you are replacing the good that Time Out can do with the harm that traditional punishment does. Mixing the bad in with the good robs Time Out of its power to teach and robs the parent of the chance to control what is being learned.

Traditional punishment tends to be so loud and dramatic that it calls attention to itself, so children focus on the spanking or noise and forget what they did to deserve it. The stronger the punishment, the easier it is to feel unjustly treated.

Time Out was deliberately designed to be quiet and mild, so children have a harder time feeling abused and an easier time remembering that it is their behavior that earns them Time Out.

Be Consistent

Let me put that another way—Always Be Consistent About Always Being Consistent.

Just as children must know that noncompliance will earn Time Out, they must know that it will earn Time Out *every* time it occurs. If they earn Time Out sometimes, but not others, then it is your decision, not their behavior, that sends them to Time Out. They know the rules. The only decisions to be made are theirs—will they comply, or will they go to Time Out?

In two-parent families, both parents must use Time Out every time a child fails to comply, or Time Out will not work. It is not Mom's decision or Dad's decision. Children must learn that they get what they earn, just as they do in real life.

Never Threaten Time Out

Just use it. Threatening teaches children that they can get away with anything at least once because they do not have to accept responsibility for what they do. When you threaten, it is your tolerance level, and not your children's behavior, that determines if they earn Time Out.

Getting the Cat Into the Bag

To the child, Time Out will seem like a game at first, much better than being yelled at or spanked. But after willingly serving Time Out for a while, Ken may decide it's time to test the system. Then getting him into Time Out can be a challenge, something like getting a dry cat into a wet bag. He knows he isn't going into that bathroom for anybody, so he isn't likely to be impressed when Mom starts adding minutes.

But Mom is determined to maintain control, so instead of yelling or beating Ken, she very calmly finds a padlock and locks up his bike. Or she turns off the television, or puts away the video game. The lock stays on, or the TV stays off, until Ken has served Time Out.

It doesn't matter how much time Ken accumulates before he starts losing privileges. Children can survive for as long as two hours in Time Out without undue suffering. What does matter is that Mom maintains her control. She needs to get out the lock as soon as she feels that she is about to lose control of herself.

Responsibility seems like a heavy load when it is carried for the first time, so children who are earning Time Out often try to bait their parents back into hitting and yelling. But once Time Out is established, resistance can easily be controlled by adding time or withholding privileges. The parent who takes control only needs to be consistent to maintain control.

Delayed Time Out

Time Out is most effective when it is used immediately after noncompliance. But in the real world, buses and teachers and preachers operate on set time schedules, and five minutes is sometimes a luxury we can't afford. If children earn Time Out while you are rushing to get them ready for school or church, you can delay it until they get home. Then they serve their time before they do anything else. Time Out is less effective when it is delayed, but delayed Time Out is still better than traditional punishment.

Time Out for Toddlers

For children age two and younger, the bathroom is not a good place to spend time alone. It's Adventureland, with wild, raging toilet bowls to be explored and towering countertops to be conquered. The danger is real. If a child will stay in a crib, then the crib is the place to spend Time Out—after all the blankets, toys, and stuffed creatures are removed.

Crib-bound children will have forgotten what all the fuss was about by the time they stop crying, so a timer is not much help. Let them decide when Time Out has ended. When they are quiet, retrieve them and repeat your original request.

Other than that, Time Out is the same for toddlers as for ten-year-olds. I ask Rosemary, age two, to pick up her blocks, but she refuses, so I calmly carry her to her crib. When she is quiet, I get her and again ask her to put the blocks away. The choice is hers—she can comply or go back to her crib. I won't wait until she's sixteen to begin teaching her to speak. Why should I wait to begin teaching her to behave responsibly?

Time Out Will Not Work When . . .

1) Time Out will not work when you do not use a portable timer. The bell, not the parent, must tell the child his time is up. The child's behavior leads to Time Out; the bell signals when Time Out is over.

2) Time Out will not work when you do not use the bathroom. If the bathroom is in use, you could use an alternative spot such as an out-of-the-way corner or laundry room.

3) Time Out will not work when you pair it with traditional punishment. You must stay calm and stop trying to force children to comply. They are responsible for their own behavior, and they will get what they earn.

4) Time Out will not work if you are not consistent in using it. The child must know in advance what things will lead to Time Out, and that they will *always* lead to Time Out.

5) Time Out will not work if you threaten it instead of using it. If you threaten, in effect you are rewarding the child for misbehavior. Judy soon learns she can misbehave two or three times before she has to face the consequences.

6) Time Out will not work if one parent uses it and the other doesn't. Both parents must agree on what behavior deserves Time Out, and must use it consistently.

7) Time Out will not work if you don't explain it before you use it. There are rules for acceptable behavior, but there are no surprises.

To Spank or Not to Spank

Any discipline should be used as a teaching tool. Before you spank, ask yourself, "What am I teaching my child?"

Reasons for Spanking

1. Spanking helps the parent release frustration.
2. Spanking is used when parents don't know what else to do.
3. Spanking stops bad behavior immediately.

Reasons for Not Spanking

1. Spanking does not result in a permanent behavior change.
2. Spanking damages the child's self-image.
3. Spanking may damage a parent's self-image.
4. Spanking sets a poor example (if you are bigger, you can hit).
5. Spanking is often directed at the child, even though the parent is angry at someone else.
6. Spanking can become uncontrollable and child abuse can begin.
7. Spanking is habit-forming.
8. In a world of violence, parents need to teach better ways to cope.
9. Spanking causes resentment. Children often want to get even.
10. Spanking can cause emotional problems (bedwetting, school failure, whining, etc.).
11. Some children are rewarded by the attention they get when they are spanked.

10

The Power of Rewards

The day after report cards came out, Mrs. Smith called me with some good news.

"Mary's doing better in school than she ever has."

"What happened?"

"Last term, she got all Ds, except for a C in math. So we did what you suggested and celebrated the C—you know, ice cream, a trip to the movies, the whole bit. This time she got all Cs, except for Math. She got a B in Math. Can you believe that?"

I could believe it. Behavior that is rewarded tends to be repeated. But behavior that is not rewarded is not likely to be repeated. When better grades earn ice cream and bad grades are ignored, all grades get better.

Later that same afternoon, Mrs. Flink called me with some bad news.

"Sandy's doing worse in school than she ever has."

"What happened?"

"Well, last term she got all Bs, except for a C in math. Of course we were upset by that C. We scolded her and grounded her—we even took her bike away for a week. But this time she did worse—all Cs, except for Math. She got a D in Math. Can you believe that?"

I could believe it. Behavior that is rewarded is repeated, even when it is rewarded with negative rewards. But behavior that is not rewarded is not going to be repeated. When bad grades earn negative rewards and better grades are ignored, all grades get worse.

Whether the behavior is wanted or unwanted, whether the rewards are positive or negative, the principle always works: behavior that is rewarded is repeated; behavior that is not rewarded is not repeated.

Many parents have problems because they work backwards, rewarding behavior that they want to stop and ignoring behavior they want to continue. Only when those parents begin to control the rewards they give do they begin to control their child's behavior.

The most powerful parenting tool I can offer you is the ability to control the rewards you give your children. The next two chapters will teach you some effective ways to reward behavior you want. But you also need to stop rewarding behavior you don't want.

Negative Rewards

Negative rewards are all those scoldings and spankings and other nasty things parents throw at their children. To parents, they hardly seem like rewards at all. But to a child who wants attention, a scolding is at least better than no attention at all, and to a child who wants power, the power to turn Mom and Dad into hysterical tyrants is reward enough to make the day.

"I've screamed at Kevin until I was blue in the face," a father told me. "But it hasn't done a bit of good. I think he just tries to make me mad."

"What would you do if someone screamed at you?"

"I'd make them sorry, you can bet!"

"Suppose it was your boss?"

"I'd find another job. Nobody's going to treat me that way."

"Well, Kevin's only six, so what's he going to do? He can't find another father. How can he get even?"

"By making me mad?"

"By making you mad."

Even when negative rewards do seem to work, they work for the wrong reasons. If you teach Steve to behave out of fear, what does he learn? He learns fear, of course, and fear is better suited to retreat than to progress.

Negative rewards teach him that it's Mom's or Dad's job to control his behavior. When he begins to ask "What can I get away with?" instead of "What's the best thing for me to do?" he has learned to be irresponsible.

Positive rewards, properly given, are always effective in controlling behavior, teaching responsibility, and building a child's self-image. Negative rewards may or may not control behavior, but you can count on them to destroy self-image and teach irresponsibility.

Positive Rewards for Negative Behavior

"Why does Harry always throw tantrums?" The parents who asked me that were convinced that they were stuck with a bad-tempered kid and there was nothing much they could do about it.

"Harry throws tantrums because you taught him to throw tantrums." That wasn't what they wanted to hear, so I went right on. "When does he throw tantrums?"

"Whenever he wants something we don't want him to have."

"What do you do when he has a tantrum?"

"Well, he won't stop until we give him what he wants."

"You've trained him well, haven't you?"

"Trained him? What do you mean?"

"When behavior is rewarded, it occurs again. Harry throws a tantrum. You reward him for his tantrum by giving him what he wants. Next time he wants a cookie, he throws another tantrum, because you've taught him that tantrums earn rewards."

"So what's the answer?"

"Ignoring."

Ignoring

If there is one thing you can count on, it is that children will try to get attention. If they can't get it for constructive behavior, they will get it for destructive behavior. If they don't get it at home, they will get it at school or from their friends. Attention is the most powerful reward any person can receive.

What happens when behavior is *not* rewarded? It is not repeated. What happens when behavior meant to get attention is not rewarded? It is not repeated. When your child wants attention, but you give no attention, then you are ignoring.

Behavior you might wish to ignore includes tantrums, tattling, whining, nagging, pouting, fighting, and bedtime disturbances. When you reward a tantrum, it will stop—for the moment. But it has been rewarded, so it will be repeated. Only when he learns that his tantrums no longer work will Harry start to find some other way to get what he wants.

The first thing that happens when parents start ignoring is that the behavior occurs more often. Harry has always gotten a cookie for his tantrum. It will take him a while to get over the shock of finding that his best trick doesn't work anymore. But if his parents won't give in, his tantrums will begin to subside within three days and eventually will stop.

I gave Harry's parent a list of five guidelines which will help them, or any parent, ignore attention-getting behavior until it goes away.

Don't Let the Child Get to You

Turn your back, if you can. If Harry sees you frown or bite your lip or pull handfuls of hair from your head, he may be rewarded in ways he doesn't expect, and the behavior will continue.

Say Nothing

No lectures, no scolding, no sympathy. Say *nothing*. You want Harry to think his tantrum is having no effect on you.

Avoid Physical Contact

If you have to leave the room, leave the room. Just don't touch Harry, or allow him to touch you, while the tantrum continues.

React Quickly

As soon as the tantrum starts, start ignoring it. But the moment it ends, stop ignoring. You still act as if the tantrum never happened—it's the behavior you are really ignoring, not the child. When the child resumes acceptable behavior, it is time for you to resume normal life.

Be Consistent

If you are ever going to give in to Harry's tantrum, you will be better off if you do it immediately. Otherwise, you are teaching him that if he screams long enough, he can beat you. The last thing you want to do is let him develop the stamina to scream for ten or twenty minutes.

Tattling

When Sally comes running in to report that Larry threw a rock or Linda threw a fit, she often just wants to report. Let her report. All you need to say is, "Thank you for telling me," and then ignore further tattling. She expects the same reward she has always gotten for her tattling—the power to get someone in trouble. But if you want the tattling to stop, you won't reward it.

If you think ignoring is difficult, you're right. The reason young children scream and cry so much is that a screaming child is hard to ignore. There is something instinctive that makes us want to help a crying infant, and that's good. It helps ensure that infants get what they need.

But as Harry outgrows infancy, we should expect him to outgrow his infant level of communication. We encourage that growth by ignoring his infantile behavior and forcing him to learn better ways to get what he wants.

11

Rewarding

Rewarding

When my own children were young, I used to hire the boy across the street to shovel the snow from my driveway. To see Tim attack the drifts, you would have thought that digging snow was his greatest joy. But one day his father knocked at my door.

"What's your secret?" he asked.

"What do you mean?"

"Tim would never think of shoveling our driveway, but he prays for snow so he can do yours."

"Imagine that," I said. "How much do you pay him?"

"Pay him? I buy his food and keep clothes on his back and drive him to school and put a roof over his head. Why should I pay him for shoveling snow?"

Why should Tim's father pay him for shoveling snow? Because that's the best way to get Tim to shovel snow. The few dollars the father spends will buy years of cooperation and miles of clear driveway.

Why should he pay Tim? Because as he earns money, Tim is learning things he will not learn any other way. He learns how to earn money. He learns that he is worth something. And as he decides how to spend or save the money he earns, he begins to learn something about responsibility.

Is he learning to be materialistic? I hope so. How else is he going to survive in a materialistic world? He is learning that it pays to be useful, and that will help him grow into a useful adult.

For richer or poorer, for better or worse, we live in a materialistic society. Some consider that a curse. But for those who know how to work for rewards, free enterprise is a great blessing. Those who contribute more get more of the rewards. Those who do less get less. That's basically how the system works.

Would you like to leave your children an inheritance to set them up for life? Then teach them how to work for material rewards. Teach them that what they get will depend upon what they do. But don't forget to teach them that money itself is only one part of a balanced life.

Balance

If your children get plenty of exercise but live on candy bars, they won't be as healthy as they could be. If they eat well but get most of their exercise at the dinner table, they won't be as healthy as they could be. Physical health requires a balance.

Emotional health also requires a balance. When they earn your praise and attention, your children will know they are richly loved. But if they don't learn about the material side of life, their lives will be out of balance and they won't be as rich as they could be.

By letting your children earn material rewards, you are preparing them for adulthood when they will be expected to provide for themselves. But if all they earn is money, they will be out of balance and their lives won't be as rich as they could be. To live without love is to live in emotional poverty, and that is much harder to overcome than material poverty.

Even parents with no money to give can give valuable rewards. If all you have to give is your time—time for a game after dinner, time to let your three-year-old help you mix up the pancake batter, time to sit and listen—you have all you need to reward your children and shape them into the kind of people you want them to become.

The most effective system is a balance of material rewards, physical contact, and praise. As Tim puts his snow shovel away, his father might hand him a dollar, put his arm around Tim's shoulders, and say, "You did a good job! Thanks."

The dollar gets Tim's attention and prints the reward more solidly into his memory, the praise tells him he is accepted and appreciated, and the hug reminds him that he is loved. Together they work to give him a healthy balance in his life.

Allowances

I had explained to Mrs. Weller how she could use money as a reward to win her daughter's cooperation. But two weeks later she was back to tell me that it didn't work.

"I started paying Sheila," she said. "But she still won't lift a dishrag. All it has done is give her money to waste on candy."

"When do you pay her?" I asked.

"Every Saturday she gets two dollars."

"Whether she works or not?"

"I told her she had to help to get the money."

"But you still pay her, whether she works or not?"

"Yes, I guess so," she admitted.

Would you work if you got paid for staying home? The idea isn't to give children money. The idea is to give them the chance to earn money.

"If you reward Sheila for doing nothing, she will continue to do nothing. A weekly allowance teaches her to accept welfare. It teaches her that money comes easily and doesn't mean much, because it doesn't have to be earned."

"Then when should I pay her?"

"Pay her when she earns it."

Payment for Performance

Two weeks later, Mrs. Weller was back. "Every night I give Sheila a quarter for washing dishes, and I let her know what a great job she is doing. But am I going to have to pay her for the rest of her life? She already seems to be losing interest."

"It's become a job to her, with a regular paycheck. I don't have to tell you how boring that can be. And it's time you start weaning her away from the quarter, anyway. So tonight, instead of giving her the usual quarter and pat on the back, surprise her. Tell her that she's been doing such a great job with the dishes, you want to send her to that movie she's been wanting to see."

"Hold on! Instead of a quarter, now I have to give her movie tickets? You call that inflation, don't you?"

"No, I call it surprise, and that's the most powerful way to give rewards. You don't reward her every night, or every week, or every month. You *surprise* her. If she doesn't know when she's going to hit the jackpot, her rewards will be much more interesting."

If you've been to Las Vegas, you know that the town has been invaded by one-armed creatures. Slot machines grin at you between the bags of dog food in the grocery stores. They welcome you to hotels and restaurants and restrooms. No matter where you go in Las Vegas, you are seldom more than an arm's length from a slot machine.

Why? Because people put money into them. We all know that they take in more silver than they give out, but still we play them. Why? Because they surprise us.

Put in your quarter, pull the handle, watch the wheels spin. No luck? Try another quarter, and another, and another. Finally the lights flash and the coins flow. Surprise! It doesn't matter that we're giving more than we're getting. As long as they surprise us often enough, we will keep feeding those slot machines.

Behavior that is rewarded with a surprise will continue, even after the rewards stop coming. There is always the chance of another payoff, and there is always the memory, made stronger by the surprise, of rewards already earned. You want Sheila to keep washing dishes, so surprise her.

If the behavior starts to slip, it's time for another surprise. Meanwhile, move your child along to new accomplishments, using the same method we used to teach Sheila to wash the dishes:

Make Children Earn Their Rewards

Allowances teach kids to do nothing to earn their money.

Establish Behavior By Rewarding Each Performance

Children need to learn that life's material rewards come to those who are useful.

Maintain Behavior with Surprises and Continued Praise

Continue to be generous with your praise, but instead of giving consistent rewards, surprise the child with a material reward. The surprise will nail down the behavior, and then you will be ready to start over with something new.

A Bird on the Plate . . .

I hadn't been married very long when Valentine's Day came along. Since I was busy with school and wasn't sure what to buy, I gave my wife a ten-dollar bill and told her to pick out some candy and flowers. She smiled sweetly, and I thought I was onto something good. I had another ten for her on her birthday, and had already decided she deserved a twenty for Christmas.

Then one Friday in November she left to spend the weekend with her parents. I studied late that night, and came home tired and hungry. But my wife had remembered me—I found a note on the table saying my dinner was in the oven.

With an empty stomach and a watering mouth, I grabbed a hotpad and set the covered plate on the table. As I found some silverware and poured myself a glass of milk, I tried to guess what was on the menu—"Roast beef with mashed potatoes? Spaghetti? Doesn't smell like spaghetti. Fried chicken? I hope it's fried chicken."

In one hand I held a fork; with the other I lifted the cover. On the plate lay two crisp, piping hot dollar bills and another note—"Dear, I couldn't decide what to get you for your dinner, so I thought I'd let you pick something out for yourself."

I got the message. Sometimes a bird on a plate is worth two at the market. And although children can learn to value money, many times a toy or a treat is twice as rewarding as the money it costs.

There are only two secrets to giving tangible rewards. First, you have to get them in advance, or you will end up giving money or promises instead. And you need to know your child well enough to select an appropriate reward. Aaron's outgrown rattles, but he's not ready for roller skates. Sharon hates baby dolls, but she'll love that bulldozer.

The shelves of the stores are stocked with everything from penny candies (at a nickel each) to books to computer software. If you take a few minutes to select the right reward, then select the right time to give it, you will find that material rewards are worth twice their cost in shaping your child's behavior.

Charting

"Mark wets his bed every night," his mother told me. "Do you think it would hurt if I made him wear a diaper to bed?"

"Why don't we just teach him to stay dry?"

"I tried. There's no way."

I couldn't argue with that, so I reached under my desk for my box of toy cars. Six-year-old Mark leaned forward to see what I was up to. He almost fell off his chair when I dumped 100 cars on the floor.

"Do you like cars, Mark?" I carelessly raked through the pile with my fingers as I spoke.

"You bet!"

"I'll tell you what. If you can stay dry one night next week, I'll give you your pick. Could you do that?"

"You bet!"

"Good." I found a piece of paper and marked a section for each day of the week. Then I labeled the days and handed the paper to Mark. "Now, whichever night you stay dry, you get to draw a smiling face on this chart. Bring it back next week and show me the face, and you can choose your car."

Did it work? It always works, because I make it work. If Mark can't stay dry one night, then I lower it to half a night, or two hours, or one hour—whatever it takes for him to earn a reward.

I want him to succeed so I can reward him, because I know that success builds on success. If he can have one dry hour this week, he can have two hours next week, and a dry night the week after. I use the chart to remind him of the task, and then to remind him of his success.

Charting is the best way I know to keep track of progress when you are teaching your child any new behavior. I always follow these rules, and charting has never failed me:

Keep It Positive

I didn't tell Mark not to wet his bed. I told him to stay dry. We're not trying to avoid failure, but working to achieve success.

Keep It Simple

Define the goal, keep it within the child's reach, and be specific enough to avoid argument. "Did Judy clean her room?" is a question with many answers, since we won't all agree on what a clean room is. Instead, ask, "Did Judy pick up her dirty clothes?" She can't meet your expectations until she knows exactly what they are.

Define Rewards

"Bill, each day you do your homework, you get to draw a smiling face. When you have five, I'll buy you an ice cream cone. When you earn ten, I'll take you to a movie."

Reward Often

If Sherry can collect a hundred smiling faces before she earns her reward, then she didn't need charting in the first place. You need to lead her along, step by step, giving small rewards for every five smiling faces on her way to a larger reward for a larger accomplishment.

Let The Child Be Responsible

Martha may choose to work for a reward, or she may choose not to. You can't force her, or threaten her, or manipulate her and expect to make any progress.

If you choose rewards she wants and keep them within her reach, she will perform.

Gradually Raise Your Expectations

Once a behavior has been mastered, replace it on the chart with a new one. You want to teach a pattern of growth and improvement that your child can follow for life.

Date Charts And Save Them

Parents get frustrated and discouraged. When it seems you are getting nowhere, it helps if you can look back and see where you have been and how far you have already come.

Display Current Charts

Magnets were invented so charts could be kept on refrigerator doors. Seeing the chart reminds both you and the child that there is work to be done and rewards to be earned. Seeing the smiling faces accumulate reminds you both that you are making progress.

Hour Charts

When I built my house, it was on a lot covered with stones—not large stones, but many stones. I decided that the way to get rid of the rocks was for my children to gather them into piles, from which I could load them into my pickup and haul them away. My children decided that they would rather learn to live with the rocks.

So I sat down at the kitchen table and drew hour charts by numbering sheets of paper from one to one hundred. Each time a child worked an hour helping around the house, he got to draw a circle by the next number on his chart, with a half-circle for a half-hour and a quarter-circle for a quarter hour.

When I explained the system to my children, they yawned and shrugged and started to walk away.

"Did I mention that anyone who works one hundred hours gets a new ten-speed?" I asked them. I must not have mentioned it, because now they rushed back to the table.

"And did I mention that picking up rocks earns double time? For each hour you pile rocks, you get to mark two hours off your chart."

I did give smaller rewards along the way, and every child made it to one hundred hours within two months. Nowadays, if I need a rock I have to borrow it from the neighbors. I can't find one on my land. It cost me three new bicycles to get those rocks picked up, but it saved my back and taught my children things that will prove priceless someday.

Success breeds success. The way to teach children to succeed is to let them succeed, and the way to tell them they have succeeded is to reward them. Your child learned to speak by saying small words at first, although not always saying them perfectly, then moving on to larger and larger words. A child learns to succeed by accomplishing small things, though not always performing perfectly, then moving on to larger and larger accomplishments.

And as success builds on success and is rewarded each step of the way, the rewards begin to pile up. If Alan earns a Frisbee for cleaning the garage, that Frisbee will be there to remind him he has succeeded. If he earns a hug and a word of praise, they will endure as small pieces of the puzzle that he is putting together to discover who he is. But the reward is always the key.

12

You're a Good Kid

"Judy used to speak right up, but now her teacher says she hardly says a word in class," Mrs. Thomas told me.

"When did she change?"

"Well, about a year ago she gave a talk in church, and she didn't do very well. Ever since, she's been afraid to talk in public."

"How did she find out that she didn't do very well?"

"I guess I told her."

"What did that teach her about herself?"

"That she wasn't a good speaker?"

"Right."

No matter how good your intentions, a little bit of criticism can go a long way. Because she was told she didn't do well on a talk that nobody else remembers anyway, Judy was set back at least a year. Who can afford to pay such a price for such a trifle?

Praise is sunshine to the self-image. Its warmth helps a child grow strong and fruitful. Its light reflects in a child's face. If there is a medicine designed to heal an ailing self-image, it is praise.

Criticism is a cold frost on the self-image. It stunts growth. It is reflected back as anger and hostility and hatred. If there is one poison that is sure to destroy self-image and slow down a child's progress, it is criticism.

No matter how it is intended, criticism gives the same message—"You blew it, kid." When that message takes root in the self-image, fear starts to grow, and when fear grows, it chokes off everything else.

Cause to Praise

Once a father looked me straight in the eye and said, "But my kid never does anything I can praise."

"Never?"

"Never!"

"Does he go to school?"

"Sometimes."

"Then praise him when he does. Does he help at home?"

"Once in a while."

"Then praise him for that."

Children who are praised will do things that deserve praise. Children who are criticized will do things to earn criticism.

If you wait for your children to do some great and earthshaking deed before you praise them, you will never get the chance to praise. But if you praise them for something they do today, they will do something better tomorrow, and something even better the day after. There's no end to what they can accomplish as they get better and better because they are being praised.

In Black and White

If you spread white paint on a dark wall, you get gray. Put on a second coat and you get a lighter shade of gray, but still gray. Your third coat will begin to look white, but it will take even more paint before the dark is completely covered.

Even when your wall looks white, all you've done is cover over the darkness. Scratch away some of the paint and it will show through again.

That's about the best you can hope for when you shift your focus and begin to praise your children. Criticism has stained their self-images, and it's going to take a whole lot of praise to cover it. Even then, it's going to reappear at times, but the more you praise, the greater the effect of the praise.

You may pay twenty dollars for a gallon of paint, but praise is cheap. It's free. You can afford to spread it thick, then add another coat when the stains begin to show through.

"Good job!" Nothing else so powerful costs so little. Say those two words—say them often—and cut out the criticism, and you can make a child into anything you want.

Getting Into the Picture

A friend of mine went to Yellowstone Park last summer and brought back a picture of himself with a grizzly bear lurking in the background. He shows it to people and they want to know all about it. What did the bear do? What did my friend do? Was he afraid?

I was also in Yellowstone last summer, and I brought back a picture of myself, along with a postcard of a grizzly. People look at my two pictures and shrug. Just because the bear wasn't around to get into my picture, they think there is no connection between us.

As young Johnny lives and learns, he is assembling a photo album in his memory. One of his mental pictures shows him doing dishes for the first time. Another, recorded four hours later, shows him being praised for washing dishes. When Johnny looks back through his album, the two pictures have little impact.

But another of Johnny's mental pictures shows him mowing the lawn and being praised at the same time. He will never forget the connection between the work and the praise, because the praise came in time to get into the picture.

Behavior will always be linked in the memory to the reward it earned. But the more time that passes between the act and the reward, the weaker that link will be.

Don't take time to decide whether Johnny deserves praise. When he does something you like, tell him immediately. If you want him to repeat his behavior, don't give him time to decide for himself if the effort was worthwhile. Tell him what to think—"Johnny, I'm really proud of you for helping your brother. You're a good kid!"

Praise on Credit

The best teacher I know works with troubled kids. One of her favorite techniques is to praise a child in advance, assuming he is going to do what she wants him to.

When Joe stomps into the classroom with his fists clenched, you or I might conclude he is looking for a fight. But my friend gives him more credit than that.

She assumes he is going to behave well, and she tells him so. "Joe, you look like you're ready to get to work. Good boy!" Then she guides him to his desk and has him working on an assignment before he knows what hit him.

Children respond to praise that is given on credit. "Mike, I'm really pleased that you came home after school to change your clothes before you went out to play." Maybe Mike just came home to use the bathroom or to get his baseball bat, or maybe he has already been outside playing for half an hour.

If you want him to learn to do what you want, you can learn to create your own reality by praising him on credit. You will find him eager to earn praise that has already been given.

Before the Home Crowd

A local college basketball team usually wins only about half its games, but some of the best teams in the country hate to play it—when it's playing on its home court. No matter how much the players may stumble and fumble when they are on the road, before the cheering home crowd they're almost unbeatable.

If the crowd around your children is pulling for them, they will give their best effort. But if the crowd is hostile, laughs at their mistakes and expects them to do their worst, they are likely to fail.

You should be a cheerleader for your children. When you praise a child in front of friends and relatives, the effect of the praise is multiplied.

"Grandma, Rosey helped me clean the house today, and she did such a good job." Rosey thinks twice as much of her effort, because both you and Grandma are telling her what a great helper she is. When you think enough of your child to brag a little, the message will come through: Both Grandma and Mom think I'm good, so I must be good.

If you want to encourage behavior, praise it. If you want to ensure it will be repeated, praise it in front of someone that your child likes to impress. You've got the home-court advantage working for you, but you've got to get the crowd involved.

Poisoned Springs

Even in the driest deserts of California, you may be lucky enough to find a pool of water springing up from the sand. Some desert springs are alive with insects and ringed with the tracks of whatever animals live in the neighborhood. Others seem absolutely clear, undisturbed by any sign of life. Given your choice, which water would you drink?

If water doesn't support life, it contains poison. That clear spring that looks so inviting might quench your thirst, but the poison it carries is likely to quench your life. Water is life. Water that has been poisoned is death.

Praise means life to the self-image. But praise can be poisoned with criticism, and then it kills what we expect it to nourish.

"Stephanie's a good kid—especially when she's asleep."

"That's good that you got Bs on your report card—but why can't you get As like your sister does?"

Anytime you add a word of criticism to a word of praise, the praise will have no effect. In fact, the mixture is one of the most destructive, confusing things you can do to a child.

If you are going to praise, then pour on the praise, expecting to build the child up. If you are going to criticize, expect to tear the child down. But when you add criticism to your praise, you are poisoning the spring, turning something healthy into something destructive.

You'll live longer with no water than with poisoned water. Children do better with no praise than with praise mixed with criticism. Why confuse them? When they know they are good, they get better. When they know they are bad, they get worse. But when they don't know what they are, they have been poisoned, and something inside starts to die.

How to Praise

Start Now and Start Small

Praise children for what they can do now, and they will be able to do more tomorrow.

Be Generous With Your Praise

It's cheap, but it's powerful.

Be Quick

Praise starts losing its power almost as soon as the behavior ends.

Praise on Credit

Praise in advance, and a child will work hard to deserve it.

Praise in Front of Others

When it's shared, the value of praise is multiplied.

Don't Mix Praise with Criticism

When praise is poisoned, it destroys the child it should be building.

13

Parentcraft

Parentcraft

"I just don't have what it takes to be a parent," Mrs. Howard told me. "I never should have had kids in the first place. They deserve better than me."

"Sounds pretty bad—have you ever done anything right?"

"I had my tubes tied, but I did it too late—should have done it before I got married."

"You've never taught your children anything useful?"

"I taught them to be careful next time they choose a mother. Is that useful?"

"So what are you going to do about it?"

"What can I do?"

"You can do anything you want."

You can do anything you want. You can keep going the way you're going, and keep getting the things you're getting. You can make small changes and get small improvements. Or you can use the tools I've given you to rebuild your family. The choice is yours.

What's In It For Me?

"You've told me to give my kids money and treats and praise," Mrs. Rasmussen said. "And it sounds like a good deal—at least for the kids. I give them this, I give them that. They love it all, but what's in it for me?"

What's in it for Mrs. Rasmussen is what's in it for any parent—control. Control means you can decide you want responsible children and teach them to be responsible. Then beds get made, dishes get washed, grades improve. You have less to worry about and more time for yourself.

You will bring peace to your family, once you take control. Your children can learn to quit yelling at each other, you can learn to quit yelling at them, and you will all live more happily ever after. You can decide what kind of family life you want to live, and you can live it.

Someday your children will be old enough to choose for themselves. One decision is going to be how much of their lives they want to share with you. Sally may be only three today, but what she is learning will help her decide if she wants Mom and Dad around fifteen years from now. If you control what she learns, you can look forward to being part of her life, and her family, for as long as you live.

What's in it for you is the opportunity to build your family into the kind of family you want. Left to chance, child-raising is a chancy business, but I've given you all the tools you need to take control. Whether you use those tools or leave them rusting in the attic is going to determine how well you and your children will live your lives.

The Tool Kit

Before you begin building, take one more look into your new tool kit. Right there on top is the tool called *Planning*. Draw yourself a life map. Where do you want to go with your family life? What do you want for your children? Once you choose a goal, you will find it easier to be consistent, and you will find it easier to keep trying to move ahead when you seem to be going nowhere.

Shaping is the tool that will let you follow your map, one step at a time. It will remind you that the only place you can start is right where you are today. And it will show you that any goal is within your reach, so long as you are willing to take the first step, and then to keep stepping steadily along.

Tradition can be a powerful tool for teaching. But even more important, it builds a sense of family. Being a part of a family gives children and their parents the stability and support they need as they learn and grow.

Time Out is a tool used instead of traditional punishment to give people a chance to regain control and to learn responsibility. It works for any child, and it works for any adult. Many times parents need Time Out for themselves as much as for their children. If you feel yourself losing control, get away for a few minutes. Take a long, hot bath, or take a walk. Take all the time you need to regain your self-control.

Praise is the best tool to build self-esteem. It's cheap, but it's powerful. As you pour it on, it spreads like syrup across the self-image. A child who is praised will work to earn more praise, and children who are praised grow into adults who try more, do more, and succeed at what they do.

Rewarding is the tool you can use to control behavior—behavior that is rewarded is repeated; behavior that is not rewarded is not repeated. Parents who learn to control the rewards they give will control their children.

These tools carry a limited guarantee. If you use them as they were designed to be used, you will begin to see results quickly, probably within a few days. But if you don't use them correctly, they may not work. They have been tested on thousands of children—retarded children, problem children, even children like yours—and they always work.

The Best You Can With What You've Got

"I hit Jeff and criticize him and ridicule him," Mrs. Jones told me. "You name it, and I've done it. I'm the worst parent in the world."

"Why are you telling me this?"

"Because he's all messed up, and I need you to fix him."

"Sorry, that's not my job—it's yours. My job is showing you how you can do yours better."

"You're going to show me how to undo all the things I've done wrong?"

"No, I can't do that, either. The past is done, and there's no way we can undo it. Whatever Jeff is, right now, today, is all you have to work with. You can do things to make him better tomorrow, but you can't change what he is today."

Whatever energy you spend worrying about the past will be wasted. Why not take some of that energy and invest it in the future? What you decide to do today is going to determine what kind of children you will have tomorrow.

"But I'm too old to change the way I raise my kids," a mother tells me.

"How old are you going to be next year?"

You're not going to get any younger, but you still have the rest of your life to live. Whether that's ten days or ten thousand, why not make them the best days of your life?

The Responsible Parent

Early in our recorded history, God asked Adam if he had been eating from that forbidden tree.

"That woman you gave me made me do it," Adam said.

"But the Devil made me do it," Eve said.

After such a beginning, is it any surprise that people still try to blame their problems on someone else? And many parents teach their children that same sort of irresponsibility. Remember Cain?

Eve had a choice, and she chose to disregard the warning label and eat the fruit. It was the same type of decision people still face every day. Living is a series of choices.

And, as Eve discovered, no amount of excusing is going to let us escape the results of the choices we make. Life is a series of consequences—what we choose is what we get.

If we took Adam and Eve as role models, we would choose for today without a thought for the misery tomorrow can bring. We would teach our children one thing and expect them to learn the opposite. And when the accounts came due, we would waste what little energy we had trying to shift the blame to someone else. There is a better way.

Responsible parents have learned that what they plant today will grow tomorrow. If they plant anger, they expect to harvest anger. If they plant love, they will get love. If they plant responsibility, they will raise children who will grow into responsible adults. There's no mystery about it—what goes in is going to come out.

How Did You Learn to be a Parent?

Most of us entered parenthood without asking such basic questions as, "What does a parent have to do?" and "Am I ready to do *that*?" Somehow we felt that we were meant to reproduce, confident that in the unlikely event some small problem should arise, we would be able to handle it.

But somewhere between the first diaper change and the first tooth, our confidence began to dissolve. We began to wonder if the skills needed to produce a baby are the same as the skills needed to raise that baby into a self-sufficient, reasonably happy adult. They are not!

Should the television break (God forbid), almost everyone would want a trained television technician to fix it. And we would never trust our car to the man who hasn't earned his star. To be successful at almost any occupation, we know, takes years of training and experience. But we jump into parenting, the most important job ever undertaken, with little training and only the most limited of skills.

Where did you learn to be a parent? In school or in church? No, you learned the same way the rest of us did—by being a child who was raised by parents.

How did your parents learn to be parents? From their parents. How did your grandparents learn to be parents? From their parents. If we could travel back in time, from parent to parent to parent, we would finally meet Adam and Eve on their way out of Paradise.

But as we learn more about human behavior, and as the science of child-raising progresses, we see that parents can be in control and can build their children into the people they want them to be.

Child Building

Mr. Barnard's barn collapsed the other day. There was no earthquake, no wind, no storm. The collection of splintered boards and rusted tin could no longer support itself, so the barn just crashed to the ground.

Mr. Barnard built his barn in the same way that some parents raise their children. If he once had a design, he must have forgotten it soon after the foundation was laid. For sixteen years he continued to drag home whatever trash or scrap he found and tack it up wherever it seemed to fit. For sixteen years he worked, until his work collapsed from its own weight, and he was left with a mess to clean up.

Across the road stands another barn. This one is older, but it stands strong, as it has through twenty-seven years of winter blizzards and spring winds. The builder had a plan and he followed it from the first bucket of concrete to the last nail. Every board fits tight. Each corner is square. The roof doesn't leak. It was built with care, and it shows.

The craft of parenting is the craft of building. A child built from whatever comes along, without a plan, is likely to collapse at the slightest pressure.

But when parents build carefully, following a plan and selecting good material, their children grow into adults who can weather any emotional storm.

14

Troubleshooting

Troubleshooting

Last spring I got my car stuck in a mudhole. I pushed it and jacked it and spun the wheels, but the more I worked, the deeper it sank. Finally I realized I wasn't going to get out without some help.

There wasn't much traffic on that road, but eventually a man drove up and stopped his pickup. He jumped out and had a tow chain hooked from the back of his truck to the front of my car before I could say, "I'm stuck!"

"Let's go!" he shouted as he climbed back into his pickup. With his foot to the floorboard, full speed ahead, he jerked my poor little car up onto solid ground. The only problem was, his chain snapped up and knocked a hole in my radiator. I wasn't stuck anymore, but I still wasn't going anywhere.

"What are you complaining about?" he asked when I showed him the pool of antifreeze under my car. "You're out of the mud, aren't you?"

As I sat beside that road and waited for a wrecker, I wished I was back in the mud. Whether your problem is with a car or with a child, doing nothing is always better than doing something to make the problem worse.

Spanking, criticism, punishment—these solutions might jerk children out of whatever mudholes they have blundered into. But quick, careless solutions often do damage that makes it more difficult than ever to get your children moving down the road you have chosen for them.

Children cause problems because they want something but don't know a constructive way to get it. Effective problem solving teaches children better ways to get what they're after. That approach is not always as quick and not always as dramatic as parents may want, but it is the only way to solve problems without causing more problems.

Back in the Mud

"Why would anybody want to look so bad?" John Clark asked me. He was talking about his twelve-year-old son, who was wearing his hair in the latest bizarre style. "But that's not even the worst of it. He's cutting school. He's drinking beer and smoking marijuana and chain-smoking cigarettes. I'll do anything I can to help him."

He was a man of his word. When I suggested he start giving rewards and praise, he went right to work rebuilding his son's self-image.

In six months, his beer-drinking, dope-smoking, class-cutting problem child had turned himself around, and I thought I'd seen the last of him. The boy wore his hair neatly cut. Not more drinking, no drugs, fewer cigarettes, better grades—what more could a parent want?

But two months later they were back in my office. The boy had butchered his hair again, hadn't been to school in a week, hadn't missed a party in a month.

"What happened?" I asked.

"I started doing lots better, but Mom never would get off my case about my cigarettes—especially after one of her friends saw me smoking in the park. I finally decided if she wasn't going to be satisfied until I was perfect, why bother? I'll never be good enough to make her happy, anyway."

When parents expect perfection, they make the problem worse or cause new problems. When parents make children feel bad about themselves, they make the problem worse or cause new ones. When parents think problems that have been growing for years should be solved in a day, they make the problems worse or create new ones.

Problems can be solved without creating new problems. They can be solved in ways that teach children to be responsible. It's not always easy—sometimes it takes more time than you want to spend and more patience than you think you have. But when your children reach adulthood feeling good about themselves and taking responsibility for their own behavior, it will have been worth the extra effort.

The following list includes many of the most common problems parents encounter, and some suggestions for solving them in positive, constructive ways. The key is always the self-image. A poor self-image is the basis for most problem behavior, and a poor self-image always makes problems worse.

When children learn to feel good about themselves and their abilities, they become more cooperative, more loving, more lovable, and more productive.

Alcohol Abuse:

Causes: Tradition, peer

pressure, and rebellion all contribute, but alcohol problems are generally self-image problems.

Things that won't work: Punishment, grounding, shaming, criticism. Anything you do to damage the self-image will make alcohol abuse more likely. Anytime you get upset or do anything else to make a child's rebellion more powerful, the rebellion will continue.

Things that will work: Teaching traditional values and your good example will help your child learn a rational approach to alcohol. Giving praise and rewards to repair the self-image is the best insurance against alcohol problems.

See: Chapter 5, "Tradition," if alcohol is a traditional problem in your family; chapter 8, "The Dragon Outside the Door," for some help in handling threatening problems such as alcohol abuse; chapters 11 and 12 for the most effective ways to build a self-image with praise and rewards.

Anorexia Nervosa:

Causes: Unknown, but social pressures to be thin contribute to the problem. The child's system eventually shuts down, and the appetite stops working. Anorexics often become more active and burn more calories, which aggravates the problem. Watch for underweight teenagers, teenagers who won't eat or who want to eat alone. Other signs include social withdrawal, hostility, and increased activity, often beginning in puberty.

Treatment: This is a life-threatening problem. Treatment must be under the close supervision of a physician and psychologist.

Arguing:
(sassing, talking back, mouthing off)

Causes: Poor self-image, poor relationship with parents, children having been rewarded for obnoxious behavior.

What won't work: Arguing, punishing, criticizing, threatening. You can't teach a child not to argue if you argue. You can't teach children to respect you if you make them feel bad about themselves, or if you let them upset you. You can't reward the child for arguing and expect the arguing to stop.

What will work: Consistently enforce your decisions, using Time Out if necessary. Reward and praise children for cooperative behavior, and ignore them when they want to argue. You can't win an argument with a child—just by joining in you give the child the power to upset you, and you lose.

See: Chapter 9, "Crime and Punishment," for effective use of Time Out; chapter 10, "The Power of Rewards," for a discussion of ignoring; chapter 5, "Tradition," for help in strengthening family ties.

Asthma:

Causes: Allergies, often caused or made worse by emotional problems and anxiety.

Treatment: In order to have effective treatment, both the physical and psychological needs must be met. Treat anxiety by working on the self-image with praise and rewards. Treat physical symptoms with the help of a physician.

See: Chapter 4, "I Told You So!" for a discussion of the importance of the self-image; chapters 11 and 12 for a description of how praise and rewarding can contribute to a good self-image, which is the best cure for anxiety.

Bedtime Disturbances:
(resistance to going to bed)

Causes: Desire to manipulate or get attention from parents.

What won't work: Nagging, threatening, spanking, scolding. If you give a child attention or power, the behavior will continue. If you damage the self-image, more serious problems will develop.

What will work: Allow children to lie in bed and read, or play quietly in the bedroom. Reward them and praise them for cooperative behavior. If the issue of sleep loses its power to upset parents, children will get the sleep they need. If your children repeatedly get up to get a drink of water or go to the bathroom, let them earn Time Out the second time they get up.

See: Chapter 9, "Crime and Punishment," for a discussion of Time Out; chapters 10–12 for help with rewarding and praising.

Bedwetting

Causes: Anxiety or depression, immaturity or lack of toilet training. Tends to run in families.

What won't work: Shaming, spanking, limiting intake of water at bedtime, waking the child up in the night. All of the above treatments take the responsibility away from the child and give it to the parent. Also, criticism or anything else that damages the self-image can increase the anxiety or depression and make the problem worse.

What will work: Rewards for staying dry, charting, praise. Believe that the child really does want to stay dry and please you. Help the child progress gradually, and use charting to reward success.

See: Chapter 3, "One Step at a Time," for a discussion of the gradual nature of progress; chapter 11, "Rewarding," for how to use charting, specifically for bedwetting.

Breath Holding:

Causes: Learned behavior designed to get attention, especially during a tantrum.

What won't work: Placing the child in a cold bath, slapping the child's face, or giving attention in any way. Any attention you give will reward the behavior, and behavior that is rewarded is repeated.

What will work: Ignoring. Attention-getting behavior stops when it is no longer rewarded.

See: Chapter 10, "The Power of Rewards," for specific steps to help you use ignoring successfully.

Chores:

(reluctance to help with work at home)

Causes: Bad attitude, poor self-image, poor family relationships, poor training, lack of motivation.

What won't work: Threatening, punishment, nagging, grounding. If you try to force cooperation, you will never get willing helpers. Slave labor is not the most effective labor.

What will work: Rewards and praise. Children can learn to help willingly, if they are rewarded and praised for helping. Begin by rewarding the effort. If you expect perfection, you are going to get resistance.

See: Chapter 3, especially the six steps for teaching children to help with housework; chapters 11 and 12 for the most effective ways to give rewards and praise; chapter 5, "Tradition," for help in building a closer family.

Drug Abuse:

Causes: Peer pressure, poor self-image, anxiety, poor parental example with alcohol and drugs.

What won't work: Punishment, shaming, criticism, threats. Drug problems equal self-image problems. Anything that makes children feel worse about themselves makes drug abuse more likely.

What will work: The child must learn to feel good about his place in his environment, and secure in his family, school, and peer relationships. Praise and reward what the child does right in every area of life, not just those relating to the problem. Ignore minor infractions.

See: Chapter 8, "The Dragon Outside the Door," for suggestions for solving many problems, including drug abuse specifically; chapters 10-12 for how to use rewards and praise to build a child's self-image.

Fighting with Brothers or Sisters:

Causes: Poor self-image, depression, jealousy.

What won't work: Yelling, spanking, threatening. Violence never cures violence. Frustration never cures frustration. Screaming parents are in no position to teach children a rational approach to problem solving.

What will work: Let your children learn to work out their own problems, and reward their cooperative behavior. The family is the best place to learn to get along, and children who can solve problems with other children grow into better husbands or wives, more effective bosses or employees. Put a stop to hitting or other physical violence by using Time Out.

See: Chapter 9, "Crime and Punishment," for an explanation of Time Out; chapter 10 for steps in controlling behavior by controlling the rewards you give; chapters 11 and 12 for ways you can repair damaged self-images by giving rewards and praise.

Homework:

(resistance to doing, failure to complete)

Causes: Irresponsibility, poor self-image, lack of motivation.

What won't work: Nagging, threatening, punishing, close supervision. As long as parents take responsibility for irresponsible children, the children can never learn to take responsibility for themselves.

What will work: Praise, positive rewards, charting, Time Out. Children will perform better when they are allowed to choose for themselves. Parents can influence the choices their children make by offering rewards and praise for completing work, and by seeing that children earn Time Out for failure to do homework.

See: Chapter 2, "Ready or Not," for a discussion of readiness and an explanation of the benefits of a positive approach; chapters 10 and 11 for how to improve performance by controlling rewards; chapter 6, "Life Maps," for help in teaching your children that what they do today will decide what they can do tomorrow.

Hyperactivity:

Causes: May be a physical, chemical, or neurological disorder, or may be a sign of a serious emotional disturbance.

What won't work: Punishment, forcing the child to sit still. This will aggravate the emotional problem and won't help to solve it.

What will work: Improving the child's self-image. Time Out can help the child calm down. Medicine, under the guidance of a physician, is effective in treating physical disorders. Hyperactive children can learn to complete tasks through shaping, charting, and rewards.

See: Chapter 9, "Crime and Punishment," for a discussion of Time Out; chapters 10-12 for directions in giving rewards and praise and using charting; and chapter 3, "One Step at a Time," to understand the gradual nature of learning.

Hypochondria:

(exaggerating or inventing physical pains, illnesses, etc.)

Causes: Poor parent-child relationship. When children get more attention for being sick than for being well, they learn to be sick.

What won't work: Giving extra attention and love to a complaining child will reward the hypochondria and teach the child to be sickly.

What will work: Building a good self-image, rewarding good health rather than poor health, ignoring minor complaints.

See: Chapter 10, "The Power of Rewards," for tips on how to ignore effectively; chapters 10 and 11 to learn how you can control a child's behavior by controlling the rewards you give.

Lying:

Causes: Lying is a symptom of stress, usually caused by problems in the family. Children who lie are often depressed and suffering from a low self-image.

What won't work: Labeling the child a liar, shaming, and punishing all contribute to a poor self-image, which will increase the stress. Any apparent improvement that occurs will be only temporary.

What will work: When children lie, even when it would be to their benefit to tell the truth, it's a sign of emotional problems. Correcting this problem takes time, patience, and many, many rewards. Until the damaged self-image is repaired, the lying will continue. Statements of traditional values will also help—"We expect people in our family to tell the truth."

See: Chapter 4, "I Told You So!" to understand the dangers of placing negative labels on a child and the power of the self-image; chapter 8, "The Dragon Outside the Door," to learn how to rob unwanted behavior such as lying of its power; and chapters 10-12 to master giving rewards and praise.

Noncompliance:

(disobedience, refusal to meet parent's request)

Causes: Poor family relationships, poor self-image.

What won't work: Nagging, threatening, punishing, screaming. Any time you try to force a child to comply, you will get resistance, and are likely to cause more serious problems. When parents try to force children to comply, the children lose the chance to be responsible for themselves.

What will work: Time Out.

See: Chapter 9, "Crime and Punishment," especially the section on Time Out; chapter 5, "Tradition," for help in building a closer sense of family.

Masturbation:

Causes: Being human. Masturbation is rewarding, and all kids do it.

What won't work: Threats, punishment, and shaming cause guilt, anxiety, and depression and can contribute to serious, life-long sexual problems.

What will work: Ignoring. Occasional masturbation is a normal part of childhood. Children who masturbate frequently are feeling anxious, so repairing a damaged self-image can keep masturbation from becoming an obsession.

See: Chapters 10-12 for techniques that help rebuild a self-image.

Nervous Habits:

(Tics, hair pulling, nail biting, foot shaking)

Causes: Continuous, involuntary movements are a sure sign of stress.

What won't work: Shaming, nagging. If you add to the stress, you add to the problem.

What will work: Improve the self-image. A child with a strong self-image feels more in control of life and is less likely to feel stress. Try to discover the cause of the stress, and deal with the cause while ignoring the symptoms. Teach the child to relax.

See: Chapter 4, "I Told You So!" for help in understanding the importance of the self-image; chapters 10-12 for an explanation of how praise and rewards can be effectively used to improve a self-image.

Pants Messing:

Causes: Poor parent-child relationship. Poor self-image.

What won't work: Mineral oil, shame, humiliation—anything that makes children feel worse about themselves will make this problem worse. Anything that takes responsibility away from the child will teach the child to be irresponsible.

What will work: A high-bulk diet will help the child gain control. Praise will help to repair the self-image. Letting the child clean up the mess will put the responsibility on the child rather than on the parent.

See: Chapters 10-12 for a description of how parents can use praise and rewards to build self-image.

School Failure:

Causes: Poor self-image, immaturity, irresponsibility.

What won't work: Punishment, threats, any attempts to force a child to perform. Harm the self-image and you will harm a child's ability to do well in school. As long as you assume responsibility for seeing that schoolwork gets done, your children won't have to be responsible for themselves, and school grades will not improve.

What will work: Rewarding and praise are especially effective for improving school performance. They build the self-image, let the child be responsible, and provide motivation for doing well.

See: Chapter 6, "Life Maps," for help in creating a long-range plan for your child's future; chapters 10-12 for a sure-fire method for improving your child's schoolwork using rewards and praise.

School Phobia:

(really not fear of school, but fear of separation from the parent)

Causes: A child with school phobia is a child with an anxious parent who has taught the child to be anxious.

What won't work: Any attempt to keep the parent and child together—riding together on the school bus, having the parent attend school, or keeping the child at home—just reinforces the anxiety.

What will work: For a child to grow and learn in healthy ways, separation must occur. The parent should force the separation by ignoring the child's statements of fear, by charting and rewarding the child for going to school, and by allowing the child some independence in other areas of life.

See: Chapter 4, "I Told You So!" for a discussion of how parents can create problems; chapters 10-12 for ways to use charting and rewarding to control behavior.

Sexual Experimentation

Causes: Natural curiosity.

What won't work: Shaming, threatening, spreading guilt. Parents who try to inhibit natural occurences can cause problems where no problems would otherwise exist.

What will work: Teach a positive, healthy approach to sex, consistent with your own value system. Sex is a natural and necessary act, and children should be taught guidelines for appropriate sexual conduct, free from guilt or shame.

See: Chapter 8, "The Dragon Outside the Door," for help with this and other problems that may seem especially threatening.

Sleep Disruptions

(crying at night, nightmares)

Causes: Anxiety, problems

in the family; this is learned behavior meant to earn attention.

What won't work: Ridicule, punishment, letting child sleep with parents. You will escalate the problem if you increase the child's anxiety with ridicule or punishment. If you take your child to bed with you, you will be rewarding the child for disruptive behavior, and the behavior will continue.

What will work: Talk quietly and comfortingly to sleeping children, to bring them to a lighter level of sleep. It is at the deepest levels of sleep that anxieties are acted out. Work to repair self-image and relieve whatever anxieties are causing the problems. If sleep disturbances occur more than three or four times during a week and last for more than one week, they may be signs of serious emotional upsets.

See: Chapters 10-12 for a discussion of effective ways to build a healthy self-image through rewards and praise.

Smoking:

Causes: Peer pressure, family tradition, advertising pressure. Tobacco is highly addictive.

What won't work: Nagging, threatening, punishment, shaming. Cigarettes are a hard habit to break. If you weaken the child's self-image, you will strengthen tobacco's grip. If you take the responsibility away from the child, you will be making it less likely that the child can ever gain control over the addiction.

What will work: There are many cures for smoking, ranging from hypnotism to nicotine gum. Whether these or any cures are effective depends upon what goes on in the smoker's mind. For any cure to work, the person needs a strong desire backed by a strong self-image. The best you can do is accept the child and work to build self-image.

See: Chapter 3, "One Step at a Time," for insight into the day-to-day approach necessary to beat the smoking habit; chapter 5, "Tradition," if the adults in your family smoke; chapter 8, "The Dragon Outside the Door," for an effective approach to combatting peer pressure.

Stealing:

Causes: Insecurity, poor self-image, irresponsibility, poor understanding of property rights, deprivation.

What won't work: Punishment or labeling the child a thief. If you make the child more insecure, you aren't helping. If you brand the child a thief, the self-image will get the message, and stealing will continue.

What will work: Use praise

and rewards to build a strong self-image and eliminate insecurity. Teaching a child to act responsibly will make stealing impossible—responsible people are unable to steal. Time Out is one tool that teaches responsiblity.

See: Chapter 9, "Crime and Punishment," for a description of how to use Time Out; chapter 4, "I Told You So!" for a discussion of the dangers of placing negative labels on children; chapter 5, "Tradition," for an explanation of how you can build a stronger sense of family to help overcome insecurity; chapters 10-12 for the most effective ways to give rewards and praise.

Stuttering:

Causes: Stuttering is a problem of development—most kids stutter as they learn to speak. If it persists, it may be a self-image problem, a physical problem, or a combination of the two.

What won't work: Telling the child to slow down or anything else that focuses the child's attention on the problem will make the stuttering worse.

What will work: Ignore it, and it should go away. Build a strong self-image with praise and rewards. If stuttering continues past age six, speech therapy will be needed.

See: Chapter 10, "The Power of Rewards," especially the section on ignoring; chapters 10-12 for methods of building a proper self-image; Chapter 4, "I Told You So!" for an explanation of how your negative labels—"Billy is a stutterer"—will become reality.

Suicide:

(threats or actual attempts)

Causes: Depression, anxiety, family strife, poor self-image; this is an attention-getting device.

What won't work: Shaming, arguing, ridicule, panic. You're facing some serious problems here, and the last thing you want to do is make them worse. Suicide is the most fearsome of dragons—don't give it more power than it already has.

What will work: You need to express your concern and love for the child, without giving suicide more power. Threatened or attempted suicide is always a desperate scream for help. Listen to the child's needs and respond to them, without rewarding the threat of suicide. Work on building a strong self-image and teaching responsibility. When children understand that they make the decisions that affect their lives, suicide begins to lose its power.

See: Chapter 8, "The Dragon Outside the Door," for help in handling threats to your family; chapters 10-12 for help in teaching responsibility and building a self-image; chapter 5, "Tradition," for help in building a stronger sense of family.

Tantrums:

Causes: Attention-getting behavior learned in infancy when screaming was the easiest way to express displeasure.

What won't work: Rewarding the tantrum in any way—by giving in, giving attention, responding with a tantrum of your own—ensures that future tantrums will occur.

What will work: Ignoring. When tantrums no longer earn rewards, they stop.

See: Chapter 10, "The Power of Rewards," especially the sections on ignoring and on rewarding unwanted behavior.

Tattling:

Causes: Attention- or power-getting device.

What won't work: Tattlers want to feel important, like a messenger who has the spotlight for a moment. They also like the power to get someone else in trouble. If they get what they want, they will continue to tattle.

What will work: Simply say, "Thank you for telling me that," then ignore any further attempt to tattle. If Susan wants to report, let her report, but don't reward her for doing it.

See: Chapter 10, "The Power of Rewards," for guidelines that will let you ignore effectively.

Thumb-Sucking:

Causes: A carry-over from the sucking days of infancy, thumb-sucking continues because it feels good and gives a feeling of security.

What won't work: Putting mittens or tape or rat poison on the thumb, shaming, nagging, or anything else that increases insecurity or robs the child of responsibility.

What will work: Thumb-sucking is not a problem until parents decide it is. The worst that can be said about it is that it may make the teeth grow crooked. Trying to stop it can damage the self-image, and crooked teeth are easier to fix than crooked self-images. The best thing you can do for a thumb-sucking child is to ignore the thumb and work on the self-image.

See: Chapter 10, "The Power of Rewards," for an explanation of ignoring;

chapter 12, "You're a Good Kid," for ways to improve your child's self-image with praise.

Truancy:

Causes: Peer pressure, poor self-image, irresponsible behavior.

What won't work: Punishment, threatening, ridicule, suspension—how are you going to teach a child to go to school by kicking him out of school? Punishment, threatening, and ridicule add to the problem by harming the self-image. When parents or school officials take responsibility for a child's attendance, the child feels free to remain irresponsible.

What will work: Ideally, learning is its own reward. Before they realize that, children need more tangible rewards for good school performance. Parents can help make school more rewarding by praising and rewarding school attendance and by getting involved in the child's education. They can also help the child relate what is learned in school to real life.

See: Chapters 2 and 3 for a discussion of learning—a child must be ready to learn, and must learn gradually, one step at a time; chapters 10-12 for advice on encouraging and rewarding a child for improved schoolwork; chapter 6, "Life Maps," for help in showing your child that the future is coming and is affected by what we do today.

Whining:

Causes: Attention-getting device.

What won't work: Punishment, giving in—any time attention-getting behavior is rewarded in any way, it will be repeated.

What will work: Ignore whining, expecting it to get worse before it stops. Give the child more attention for speaking in normal tones, and stop giving attention when the child whines.

See: Chapter 10, "The Power of Rewards," especially the sections on ignoring and on rewarding unwanted behavior.

About the Authors

Tony LaPray is a psychologist in Salt Lake City with a busy private practice. He has served as president of the Utah Psychological Association, and he is a Diplomate in marriage and family psychology. He has also been on the faculty of three major universities and has done consulting for numerous public and private agencies. He is married, the father of five children, and he lives on a farm where he raises kids and cows.

Bob Greer is a professional writer with several periodical articles to his credit. *Help! For Parents* is his first book, and he is currently at work on three more. He is married and the father of two children.